Penn Greek Drama Series

Series Editors
David R. Slavitt
Palmer Bovie

The Penn Greek Drama Series presents fresh literary translations of the entire corpus of classical Greek drama: tragedies, comedies, and satyr plays. The only contemporary series of all the surviving work of Aeschylus, Sophocles, Euripides, Aristophanes, and Menander, this collection brings together men and women of literary distinction whose versions of the plays in contemporary English poetry can be acted on the stage or in the individual reader's theater of the mind.

The aim of the series is to make this cultural treasure accessible, restoring as faithfully as possible the original luster of the plays and offering in living verse a view of what talented contemporary poets have seen in their readings of these works so fundamental a part of Western civilization.

Aristophanes, 1

The Acharnians, Peace, Celebrating Ladies, Wealth

Edited by
David R. Slavitt *a n d* Palmer Bovie

PENN

University of Pennsylvania Press
Philadelphia

10 9 8 7 6 5 4 3 2 1

Published by
University of Pennsylvania Press
Philadelphia, Pennsylvania 19104-4011

Library of Congress Cataloging-in-Publication Data
Aristophanes.
    [Works. English. 1998]
    Aristophanes / edited by David R. Slavitt and Palmer Bovie.
       p.   cm. — (Penn Greek drama series)
    Contents: 1. The Acharnians / translated by Jack Flavin. Peace / translated
by Fred Beake. Celebrating ladies / translated by David R. Slavitt. Wealth /
translated by Palmer Bovie
      ISBN 0-8122-3456-1 (v. 1 : acid-free paper). —ISBN 0-8122-1662-8 (pbk
: v. 1 : acid-free paper)
      1. Aristophanes—Translations into English.   2. Greek drama
(Comedy)—Translations into English.   I. Slavitt, David R., 1935– .
II. Bovie, Smith Palmer.   III. Title.   IV. Series.
PA3877.A1S58   1998
882'.01—dc21   98-8446
                                                   CIP

Contents

Introduction

Ralph M. Rosen

The plays of Aristophanes collected in these volumes, composed and performed in Athens during the fifth and fourth centuries B.C., are the earliest surviving record of comic drama in Western culture. Like its contemporary and cognate form tragedy, Attic comedy seems to appear suddenly as a fully formed and remarkably complex poetic genre, paradoxically wedded to its own cultural moment yet profoundly resonant for audiences and readers up to our own time. Indeed, the seeds of Gilbert and Sullivan, the Marx Brothers, or Monty Python's Flying Circus are readily apparent in Aristophanes and can easily lead one to assume that not much has changed in comedy since antiquity. Yet the comic drama of fifth-century Athens, known as Old Comedy, was the product of a long and complex process of literary and cultural interactions and displays as many idiosyncrasies of its own age as it does links to later traditions. Behind the sprightly, colloquial translations featured in this series lie a richly varied Greek verse form and, as the following pages will show, a comic aesthetic by turns alien and familiar to our own sensibilities.

During the fifth century the Athenians would gather together twice a year to honor Dionysus, god of wine and revelry. The largest and most extravagant of these festivals occurred in early spring, toward the end of March, and was known as the Great Dionysia, or City Dionysia, to distinguish it from so-called rural Dionysia, which were celebrated on a lesser scale throughout the Attic countryside. The other festival, known as the Lenaean Dionysia (named after the Lenaion sanctuary where it was held), was a more limited, domestic affair that took place in January–February. Various activities occurred at these festivals, including processions, sacrifices, and musical competitions, but the central event at each was the performance of tragedy and comedy. Great expense and effort were lavished on these dramatic performances, as poets and actors competed for prizes awarded by a panel of judges drawn from ten tribes of Attica.

Tragedy and comedy were so much a part of a formal state event that the entire Athenian citizenry might, in principle, attend the performances. The Theater of Dionysus itself on the Athenian acropolis was evidently capable of holding about 17,000 spectators. The Lenaean Dionysia was a smaller and less prestigious affair than the City Dionysia, and theatrical performances were formalized there rather late in the century (about 440 B.C.). Even so, the Lenaea was as public an event as the City Dionysia, and the plots of Lenaean tragedy and comedy likewise reflect the poets' awareness that they were composing before the entire "national" community.

Drawing on a rich store of inherited myths and plots, the most skillful tragic poets crafted plays that could address issues central to Athenian political and social ideology—the relationship between rulers and their subjects, the nature of democracy, the interaction of man and woman, to name a few—and the result was that characteristically "tragic" blend of timeliness and universalizing. Greek comedy evolved alongside tragedy at the festival competitions and became equally implicated in its own historical moment, but, unlike tragedy, it was not constrained to work with mythological material, nor did it need to preserve a consistent and unbroken dramatic illusion. The comic poet was relatively free to invent plots out of whole cloth, and his imagination was limited only by his sense of what the audience would find acceptable. Furthermore, although it shared with tragedy basic compositional units, namely the alternation of spoken "episodes" with choral song and dance, comic diction was far less formal and stylized than that of tragedy. Old Comedy, therefore, could reflect the contemporary cultural climate much more directly than could tragedy: not only could the poet allude to current events or famous people through allegory or analogy but he could even name names, express indignation, and claim a personal authority (however disingenuously) to a degree wholly unavailable to his colleagues in tragedy.

The license afforded Attic comedy in the composition of plots and choice of language has a history that extends well beyond its institutionalization at the Dionysian festivals of fifth-century Athens. The exact origins of Attic comedy are difficult to trace, but the word *komoidia* itself, from which "comedy" derives, offers a useful starting point. *Komoidia* means a *komos*-song, where the *komos* refers to a group of men, often costumed, who entertained audiences with song and dance at various festive occasions. Modern analogues to the ancient *komos* are likely to be found in the activities of Mummers, still common in certain European and American holiday celebrations. Like Mummers, *komos*-singers (*komoidoi*) performed interactively with an audience, often humorously cajoling and mocking individuals with attitudes and language that in normal circumstances would be disruptive and transgressive. Little is known about how and when *komoi* actually became comic *drama*, formally performed before a passive audience, but the most fundamental vestige of the *komoi* in Attic comedy can be seen in the humorously antagonistic relationships so common between individual characters and groups of characters, and between poet and audience. Fifth-century comic drama preserves some of the carnivalesque spirit of the *komos*, which rendered vituperation and satirical commentary innocuous by means of humor, irony, and a basic assumption that comic speech was ultimately fictive, no matter how "real" it pretended to be in performance.

Indeed, perhaps the central dynamic of Aristophanic comedy is precisely the tension that arises between the poet's voice, with its didactic claims and autobiographical pretenses, and the fictional demands of the genre itself. Did Aristophanes write the *Clouds*, which satirizes Socrates and his followers, because he had a genuine personal animus against him, or because Socrates was an eccentric, funny-looking man who would make a great comic spectacle? Or did the poet exploit the comic potential of Socrates, not because he had anything against him personally but because he wanted to use him to register his own sincere criticism of current philosophical trends? That seems reasonable until one notes that the play itself offers very little in the way of philosophical consistency: traditional "philosophy," which the play ostensibly endorses, ends up as comically ridiculous as the newfangled, sophistic ways that it claims to repudiate through its satirizing of Socrates.

We face a similar dilemma in assessing Aristophanes' relationship with his other famous target, the demagogic politician Cleon, who is relentlessly, often violently, mocked in *The New Class*, and mentioned with disdain at least somewhere in nearly all his fifth-century plays. Aristophanes even alludes to an actual personal feud with Cleon, a feud that supposedly began when Cleon attempted to prosecute the poet for publicly ridiculing

Athenian politicians in his (now lost) play of 426 B.C., *Babylonians*. Aristophanes was very convincing: ancient commentators spoke of the feud as if it were a documented historical fact, and modern critics have followed suit, even though our only evidence ultimately comes from the comedies themselves, which have a generic obligation to create personal animosities between the poet and a target. We will probably never know for sure whether Aristophanes truly feuded with Cleon, but the question of historicity is ultimately less significant than the ways the comic poet persistently exploited the topos throughout his plays. For through the relationship with Cleon as it was developed on the stage over several plays spanning at least five years—*The Acharnians* (425), *The New Class* (424), *Clouds* (423), *Wasps* (422), and *Peace* (421)—Aristophanes could dramatize with brilliant economy the ethos of boisterous confrontation and antagonism that fueled so many plays of Attic comedy.

Any literature in which an author adopts a stance of moral indignation and undeserved beleaguerment, and engages in invective or personal mockery, makes it especially difficult for the audience to separate fiction from reality, if only because the author works hard to enlist their sympathies for his allegedly urgent and topical predicament. Yet despite this implied bond with an audience in opposition to a target, a group, or even an issue, we never witness the poet's voice directly in any of Aristophanes' plays (Dikaiopolis in *The Acharnians* is about as close as we get to this). No character ever explicitly represents the poet himself, and the poet's name is never directly mentioned. Instead, Aristophanes avails himself of a structural device known as the *parabasis*, which had become the conventional place in Old Comedy, where the poet could interrupt the flow of episodes and make personal claims through the mouthpiece of the chorus. The *parabasis*, which comes from the verb *parabaino*, "to step aside," was essentially a digression, a temporary halt in the main action while the chorus came forward to address the audience. Its location in the play was not rigidly fixed but tended to occur toward the middle of the play, often functioning as a kind of entr'acte. In its most elaborate form—as we see, for example, in *Wasps*—the parabasis consists of a prolonged exchange between the chorus and its leader, alternating spoken and sung verse, in which the chorus leader actually speaks on behalf of the poet.

Through the chorus leader, then, Aristophanes could take up any number of topics, including current events, the superiority of his comedy over that of his rivals, indignation at the audience for lack of support, and, of course, abuse against "personal enemies" such as Cleon. The parabasis is our main source for "autobiographical" information about Aristophanes and the primary reason it has always been so tempting to take a biographical approach to the interpretation of Aristophanes. When *Clouds* makes fun of Socrates or *The New Class* inveighs against Cleon, when Aeschylus defeats Euripides in the literary contest of *Frogs*, the relationship with the audience that Aristophanes establishes in successive parabases makes it easy to assume that the plots themselves functioned likewise as a coded, didactic message: Aeschylus defeated Euripides, so Aristophanes must therefore endorse this verdict and be trying to warn us against the evils of Euripides! But if *Frogs*, to continue with this example, were such a simplistic morality play, Aristophanes would hardly have ridiculed the literary excesses of *both* tragic poets with as much care as he does, nor would he have left the final decision to the waffling, delightfully buffoonish god Dionysus, who can barely offer a rationale for his final elevation of Aeschylus from the underworld.

Centuries of readers have had the same problem in trying to ascertain Aristophanes' views on politics or such social issues as gender relations. Do his attacks on Cleon indicate that he was "conservative"? Do his so-called peace-plays (*The Acharnians*, *Peace*, *Lysistrata*), which clearly articulated a longing for the end of the Peloponnesian War (a conflict between Athens and Sparta that lasted for nearly three decades, from 431 to 404), indicate the poet's disapproval of current Athenian war policy? Did the cluster of plays that highlighted women (*Lysistrata*, *Celebrating Ladies*, *The Sexual Congress*) reveal the poet to be anachronistically enlightened about women—a protofeminist? The plays can easily suggest such conclusions, but in fact no really systematic political or social outlook is forthcoming from them. Characters will take apparently clear political stands one moment in a play, only to undermine them elsewhere, usually for the sake of a good laugh. And when it comes to Aristophanes' sexual politics we must remain agnostic as to whether the power and status he affords women in some of his plots were received as a prescription for social change or as an extended joke "among the guys" who made up most of the audience.

Rather than dwell on Aristophanes' personal beliefs, which we can never hope to recover anyway, let us to focus on the politics and poetics of comic satire as a literary genre. In line with the antagonistic dynamic of such poetry and the poet's need to find in his surroundings something worthy of mockery, something that would strike a chord in an audience that was pitting his comic sensibility against that of his rivals, Aristophanes naturally gravitates to topics that generate controversy in nearly all societies: domestic and international politics, celebrity lives and their scandals, popular entertainment, education, and so forth. These are areas in which the slightest eccentricity can seem amusing, especially when exaggerated by caricature and incongruity. Any deviation from "the way things were" is always fodder for a satirist, and Aristophanes is famous for plots that dramatize the conflict between the "traditional old" and the "unconventional new," whether these dramatize old and new generations (e.g., *Clouds*, *Wasps*), political ideologies (e.g., *The New Class*, *The Sexual Congress*), or poetic styles (e.g., *Celebrating Ladies*, *Frogs*). This explains the general conservative feeling of so many of the plays, an almost wistful yearning for life to remain stable and ordered when the progress of time inevitably ensures that it cannot. This also explains why politicians then in office, for example, or philosopher-professors teaching for pay, were natural targets of comic ridicule: they existed in the here-and-now, and they had the potential to influence everyone's life. Any false step of theirs could cause intense anxiety within the demos, and one way the Athenians grappled with this anxiety was to reprocess it as comic performance. Comedy probably did little to change whatever views on political and moral issues audiences brought with them to the theater (it might seem remarkable, for instance, that, not long after Aristophanes' unrelieved attack on Cleon in *The New Class* won first prize, the Athenians elected Cleon general), but comic poetry would certainly have encouraged them to refine their perspectives on the complex ideological forces that governed their city and their own interpersonal behavior.

As a form of public art, organized and at least partially funded by the state, Old Comedy necessarily reflected prevailing cultural norms, and its success depended largely on its ability to walk the fine line between questioning—and occasionally subverting—these norms and merely endorsing them. The generally conservative tendencies of satire were no doubt ultimately reassuring to a democracy that institutionalized the comic performances to begin with. One cannot easily imagine, after all, what group would endorse an art form that seriously repudiated its fundamental claims to legitimacy, and few looking back today on the audience of Aristophanes' time would deny that Aristophanic comedy presupposes the desirability of democracy as practiced in the fifth century. Certainly the ancient testimony mentioned earlier, even if fictional, that Cleon sued Aristophanes for slandering the demos and its politicians in his *Babylonians* of 426 suggests that there were perceived limits to comic ridicule at the time. But so far as we can tell these limits were never systematically articulated or, for that matter, rigorously enforced. It was probably less the fear of any slander laws that restricted the freedom of comic poets than a finely honed sense of what the audience—the demos itself—would find humorous.

Although we possess only eleven complete plays by Aristophanes (representing perhaps a quarter of his total output), we are fortunate that these eleven offer examples of his art from every period of his career. Readers who approach them chronologically will note that the latest plays, both from the fourth century, *The Sexual Congress* (392) and *Wealth* (388), reflect changes in structure and content from those composed in the fifth century. The most conspicuous difference lies in the diminishing role of the chorus. In its earliest stages comedy, like tragedy, was as much a spectacle of music and dance as of spoken verse, and the chorus was clearly an area in which costume, song, and gesture could be combined to create a theatrical extravaganza. Eight of Aristophanes' surviving plays, in fact, take their titles from the identity of the chorus, and in all the fifth-century plays his choruses play an integral role in the plot. (*Frogs* is a quirky exception in that it has two choruses—the frogs themselves and a band of religious initiates; the frogs appear only briefly, at the beginning, and the initiates take over the choral duties for the rest of the play.) *The Sexual Congress* and *Wealth* still have choruses, but their role is, by contrast, highly restricted and at times almost obtrusive. Some of the manuscripts of these plays indicate places in the text where someone (the poet, perhaps, but we cannot be sure) was expected to add a choral song and dance as a kind of interlude. Some scholars have even suggested that these were points in the play where the chorus was expected to improvise ad libitum while the actors prepared for the next scene. The details remain uncertain, but we can say with confidence that song and dance were increasingly relegated to the sidelines, used as ornamentation and framing but no longer deemed necessary for the advancement of the plot.

Two other changes in Aristophanes' fourth-century plays throw into relief the process by which Old Comedy gradually developed into its later forms, Middle and New Comedy. First, the parabasis all but disappeared by the fourth century, and as a result the poet's carefully constructed relationship with his audience became necessarily less explicit. Second, even though the non-Aristophanic examples of Middle Comedy are fragmentary, it seems clear that the pointed satire, the personal, often obscene abuse we associate with Old Comedy was significantly softened. Both these changes are in keeping with a general fourth-century trend away from strictly topical, highly episodic plots, such as we find in Old Comedy, toward plots that display greater narrative coherence and linearity. Earlier concerns with specific events and personalities of the day slowly gave way to "universalizing" topics of human interest, which can be vividly seen in the popularity of stock comic characters—cooks, slaves, philosophers, misers, misanthropes, and so forth.

The shifts in public taste that Middle and New Comedy reflect are not easy to account for, but doubtless the dissolution of the Athenian empire after the Peloponnesian War and an internationalizing movement of culture in the fourth century are at least partly responsible. Were our evidence better for the period, we would probably find that the development of Greek comic drama, as well as its public reception, was hardly as uniform as we tend to construe it. Compare in this regard the state of comic drama in our own culture. Aristophanes' rambunctious, topical satire is reincarnated in late-night talk-shows, British series such as *Benny Hill* or *Fawlty Towers*, Gilbert and Sullivan revivals, Marx Brothers movies, and Three Stooges shorts. Yet at the same time contemporary popular taste seems generally to favor the genres that look more like Middle or New Comedy, as is clear from the fact that the situation comedy has held sway on television for several decades. No doubt the Greeks of both the fifth and fourth centuries also had the capacity to appreciate a variety of comic styles, and poets could be found to cater to all tastes. We have only scattered remnants of such poets, and only a skeletal understanding of how comedy evolved, but the literary eclecticism that Aristophanes alone displays across his entire career testifies to a poetic catholicity that would be remarkable in any age.

The Acharnians

Translated by
Jack Flavin

Translator's Preface

The Acharnians is the oldest extant comedy of Aristophanes, written when he was in his early twenties. The play won first prize at the Lenaean Festival in 425 B.C., the sixth year of the Peloponnesian War, and it is one of three peace plays that Aristophanes wrote against continuation of that war.

The protagonist of the play is Dikaiopolis, an old farmer who has been driven off his land and compelled to take refuge within the Athens perimeter by the depredations of the Spartans. Dikaiopolis, whose name literally means "good citizen," has tried in vain even to get a hearing for peace from the Athenian Assembly, where the "hawks" and war profiteers are in the ascendant. He then takes matters into his own hands and sends a personal emissary to Sparta, to conclude peace for himself and his family alone. He will then be able to carry on trade with Sparta and its allies and enjoy all the fruits of peace.

However, the Acharnians, from a district north of Athens, have been hard hit by the Spartan raids and are violently opposed to peace. They are determined to carry on the war, to the death if necessary, to avenge the loss of their vineyards. They are also determined to have the head of Dikaiopolis, whom they consider a traitor for making peace with the enemy.

As the Assembly opens, Amphitheus, the Immortal, is called but not chosen to make peace with Sparta. He is quickly cut down to size and packed off by the court officers. Dikaiopolis attempts to defend Amphitheus' efforts to have peace placed on the agenda, but is told to sit down and shut up.

The Ambassador to Persia is introduced after an absence of eleven years with a pseudo-Oriental retinue; it features the Eye of the Great King, who wears a mask with one great eye, and Pseudobogus, who speaks in tongues that only the Ambassador can understand. Dikaiopolis provides acerbic commentary as all these characters are paraded forth.

Next Theorus, the Ambassador to Thrace, is introduced. He leads an army of mercenaries from that region, and they promptly demonstrate their rapacity by pilfering Dikaiopolis' garlic, thereby ruining his lunch.

Dikaiopolis is furious at his treatment by these "circumcised barbarians," and even more because it is countenanced by the Assembly. He says that he felt a drop of rain, an ill omen, and the Assembly is quickly called on account of (possible) rain and wet grounds.

It is at this point that Dikaiopolis dispatches Amphitheus to Sparta bearing eight drachmas to sue for peace on his behalf.

Aristophanes gives free rein to his fantasy in this free-wheeling succession of satiric episodes that bump up against each other in their profusion, not unlike blackout sketches or oldtime burlesque. And it has been said that, of all Aristophanes' heroes, none is closer to his heart and to his own sentiments than Dikaiopolis. The so-called "good citizen" even speaks of having written comedies himself and refers to the lawsuit Cleon brought against the poet the previous year.

It might be noted that a synonym of the Greek word for protagonist is "champion," and Dikaiopolis does indeed champion his poet before the judges of the Festival in an effort to win the prize for his play, which, of course, he eventually does.

As a role for actors, Dikaiopolis is a dream come true. It wouldn't be surprising if the playwright, like Shakespeare, took part in plays himself in his youth. And if we consider Dikaiopolis in the light of the old humors, for instance, he is a chameleon. In the opening scene, we find him seated in the Pnyx, brooding and melancholy, awaiting the opening of the Assembly:

> How many times has life cut me to the quick?
> Too many to count. Like fleabites on an old dog.
> But then, how many times has life brought me
> any pleasure? Precious few! . . . (1–4)

But after proceedings in the Assembly begin, Dikaiopolis' mood quickly changes to choleric as he observes the rapidly changing cast of characters, most of whom Aristophanes regarded as venal or foolhardy. And, because he names names of real people who may well be sitting in the audience, we must marvel at the tolerance of the society, if not of the individuals who are pilloried.

After Dikaiopolis achieves his private truce, this quick-change artist whose very name means "good citizen" ironically turns his back apathetically on both the state and its citizenry. He drops out totally to concentrate on private pursuits and pleasure. In the end he is the very portrait of sanguinity, a cheerful man bursting with confidence, if not bawdy machismo. But, after all, isn't the pursuit of good cheer what comedy is all about?

But, beyond the pleasure principle, common sense is also one of the thrusts of comedy. The play contains Dikaiopolis' famous speech that justifies the Spartans' actions in the war as reactions to Athenian intransigence:

> . . . some of our own, a few wicked little men,
> worthless fellows with no scruples and less character,
> who began spreading rumors that the Megarans
> were importing contraband produce to the City. (484–87)

Further:

> But the real trouble began when a few tipsy
> young men went over to Megara one night
> and kidnapped the courtesan, Simaetha. The Megarans
> were cut to the quick and, in return, stole
> two girls from the house of Aspasia. So all
> of Greece went to war over three whores. (492–97)

Aspasia, the mistress of Pericles, is characterized as running a bawdy house, but Pericles was infuriated by the Megarans and promulgated the Megaran decree, which effectively cut off the Megarans from all trade with Athens. This led the Megarans to seek assistance from their protectors, the Spartans, who, when the Athenians refused to soften the decree, promptly took up arms.

Dikaiopolis has prepared for this speech, with which he will literally risk his neck on the chopping block, by visiting Euripides, who was a favorite target of Aristophanes and a frequent bit player in his plays. The tragedian is characterized as a seedy character who may even have employed a slave to write dialogue. Dikaiopolis borrows the rags and rhetoric of one of Euripides' protagonists and so feels equipped to face the Chorus of Acharnians and pull the wool over their eyes. He confesses as much to Euripides:

> . . . the Chorus will stand there gaping
> like imbeciles, while I bamboozle them
> with oratory. (426–28)

In this he succeeds by splitting the Chorus into warring factions, one of which calls on Lamachus, the cartoon character of a braggart general whom Dikaiopolis devastates thoroughly in a war of words. After Lamachus is summoned to defend the country's borders in the snowy passes, Dikaiopolis is called to dinner with the High Priest of the Festival of Dionysus:

> MESSENGER
> . . .
> Everything is prepared: couches,
> tables, rugs, wreaths, perfumes, sweetmeats,
> courtesans, and there are meal cakes, flat cakes,
> sesame and honey cakes, and lovely
> dancing girls besides. So, come quickly! (952–56)

Aristophanes sets up a marvelous comic counterpoint between Lamachus' wretched future and Dikaiopolis' bright one:

> LAMACHUS
> Boy! Boy! Bring me out my knapsack.
>
> DIKAIOPOLIS
> Boy! Boy! Bring me out my dinner chest.
>
> LAMACHUS
> Bring me the onions and salt with thyme.
>
> DIKAIOPOLIS
> Bring me a piece of fish. I hate onions.
> . . .

LAMACHUS
Bring me the plumes for my helmet.

DIKAIOPOLIS
And for me, my doves and thrushes. (960–63, 966–67)

Dikaiopolis, having achieved peace in his own time, is enable to pursue trade with Megara, where the populace is on the point of starvation. One enterprising Megaran, however, conceives the idea of selling his little daughters as suckling pigs. The trader addresses his daughters:

MEGARAN
. . . Come on, ye little darters of a poor
unfortunate father. Try and find something to eat
for yer old Dad. Now which would ye rather? To be sold
or to go hungry?

DAUGHTERS
Oh, to be sold, to be sold!

MEGARAN
I think so too, but who would be fool enough
to buy ye? I know an old Megaran trick.
I'll dress yez up as little porkers and put
yez up for sale. Put these clogs on for trotters
and no one will be the wiser ye're not blue-ribbon
little sows. Now get in these sacks and make
little pig-squealin' noises. Dikaiopolis!
Ho, there! Are ye in the market for some tender
little porkers in a poke? (681–93)

The scene is played for broad comedy with little or no regard for the plight of the Megarans. Everyone and everything is thrown into the comedy's maw: Euripides and Pericles, not to mention poor Lamachus, who re-enters in the final scene, "wounded" with a sprained ankle received when he tried unsuccessfully to leap a ditch, although the real Lamachus was apparently a brave officer who was killed in the war a few years later.

At the same time that Aristophanes' Lamachus is borne off to the infirmary, moaning and supported by attendants, Dikaiopolis reenters cavorting, triumphantly waving his wineskin, with a courtesan on each arm. All's fair in love and comedy.

However, did Aristophanes influence the course of events by bringing about the conclusion of the Peloponnesian War? It is unlikely that his plays did much to sway the populace other than to laughter, because the war continued until 404 B.C., twenty-one years after production of *The Acharnians*.

With regard to this translation, although it is virtually impossible to reproduce the bawdy gusto and free-wheeling improvisation of the original, not to mention the conveyance that moves it so irresistibly, the poetry of Aristophanes, an effort has been made to give the actors words they can speak on a modern stage.

Cast

DIKAIOPOLIS
HERALD
AMPHITHEUS
AMBASSADOR to Persia
PSEUDOBOGUS
THEORUS, envoy to Thrace
CHORUS of Acharnian Elders
WIFE of Dikaiopolis
DAUGHTER of Dikaiopolis
CEPHISOPON, servant of Euripides
EURIPIDES
LAMACHUS
MEGARAN
GIRLS, daughters of Megaran
INFORMER
BOEOTIAN merchant
NICHARCHUS
SERVANT of Lamachus
ATHENIAN farmer
BRIDESMAID
MESSENGER to Dikaiopolis and Lamachus
NONSPEAKING
    Commissioners, officials, citizens
    Other ambassadors to Persia
    Eunuchs: Kleisthenes and Straton
    Thracian troops
    Servants of Dikaiopolis: Xanthias and another
    Ismenas
    Musicians
    Courtesans

*(In the background are three houses: the middle one is that of
Dikaiopolis, the other two are those of Euripides and Lamachus.
In the foreground is the Pnyx, where Dikaiopolis is awaiting the
opening of the Assembly.)*

DIKAIOPOLIS
How many times has life cut me to the quick?
Too many to count. Like fleabites on an old dog.
But then, how many times has life brought me
any pleasure? Precious few! Four,
    as a matter of fact . . .
(smiles, remembering)
                    But how it warmed the cockles
of my heart when the Knights made that chiseler
Cleon cough up the bribe. Five talents!
and sweat blood besides. It made me proud
to be a Greek!
                    But wait, how about the day
I went to the theater, all agog to hear   10
the deathless words of Aeschylus? What
did I hear instead? An announcement: "Bring out your play,
Theognis!" Theog-Who? I was in shock for a week.
And Moschus, another hack, could light up a room
just by leaving it.
                    But what a joy it was
to hear Dexitheus play the lyre, the sweet
strain of Boeotian melodies. This year,
though, at the competition I almost broke
my neck to escape when Chairis poisoned the air
with his flute. But nothing since I was wet behind   20
the ears has griped me like this. Here it is,
Assembly Day, and no one's here. They should
have come at dawn. Yet the Pnyx is empty.
They're all out gabbling, rumor-mongering,
up, down, and around the Agora.
Anything, anything at all to dodge
their civic duty and not get nailed for fines.
Even the Commissioners aren't here yet.
Oh, they'll get here all right at the last minute,
falling all over each other, pushing and shoving   30
for front-row seats. But to discuss the war

and bring peace to the land? FORGET ABOUT IT!
They're out to lunch. Ah, Athens, Athens,
I'm always the first one here, bitching and moaning,
groaning with boredom, twiddling my thumbs. What
shall I do now? Take off my shoes and twiddle
my toes?
        Oh, Zeus, how I hate the city.
Buy this! Buy that! Over here!
Mine is better! In the country, it's all
there for the taking. Oil, vinegar, whatever.   40
There's never a shortage of charcoal in the village.
So here I sit, ready to start a riot,
heckle them all to death if they dare to discuss
anything but peace.
(Enter Commissioners, officials, and citizens.)
        But here they come now,
the Noon-Day Boys, the Out to Lunch Bunch.
And just as I said, all elbows and knees,
to jockey for position. Everyone wants to be
numero uno.

HERALD *(entering)*
        Move up, move up, everyone!
And stay in consecrated ground behind the lines.

AMPHITHEUS *(entering breathlessly)*
Has the speaking begun?   50

HERALD
Who wishes to address the Assembly?

AMPHITHEUS
I do!

HERALD
        And who are you?

AMPHITHEUS

                    Amphitheus the Divine!

HERALD
    You're not mortal?

AMPHITHEUS

                    You've got it, I'm immortal.
(continues pedantically)
    Now the first Amphitheus was the son of Demeter
    and Triptolemus. And *their* son was Celeus,
    who married Phaenarete. And Phaenarete
    was my father's mother. And so you see, I'm divine.
    and the gods have commissioned me, and me alone,
    to make peace with Sparta. Unfortunately,
    although I'm divine, I'm short at the moment,   60
    and the Commission has turned me down for travel money
    to Sparta.

HERALD
                    And so you're Amphitheus the Short, then?
    Officers, out with him!

AMPHITHEUS *(being dragged out)*
                        Triptolemus, Celeus!
    Where are you when I need you?

DIKAIOPOLIS *(addressing the Commissioners)*
    You're doing wrong here!
    You're violating the Assembly by hauling away
    this man, who only wants to stop the war
    and bring peace.

HERALD
                    Silence! Take your seat!

DIKAIOPOLIS
    By Apollo, I will not, unless peace is on the agenda.
*(Enter, clad in gorgeous Oriental apparel, the envoys sent to the Persian
                court eleven years earlier, during the archonship of
                Euthymenes.)*

HERALD
    PRESENTING THE AMBASSADORS FROM THE KING OF
                KINGS!   70

DIKAIOPOLIS
    The King of what? I'm fed up with ambassadors
    strutting around like peacocks.

HERALD
                                        Silence, there!

DIKAIOPOLIS
    Holy smokes! It's a floorshow from Never-Never Land!

AMBASSADOR
    In the days when Euthymenes was Archon, you
    despatched us as envoys to the Persian King of Kings.
    We had to make do, pinching obols
    where we could, on two drachmas a day.

DIKAIOPOLIS
    Ye gods, eleven years! The drachmas!

AMBASSADOR
    It was difficult, but someone had to do it.
    I tell you, reclining on those litters of down,   80
    getting lugged across the plains, never
    getting any sun under the awnings,
    and the slaves with their cursed fans! It was *hard*.

DIKAIOPOLIS
   While I reclined in rubbish up to my armpits on the parapets.

AMBASSADOR
   And they were forever wining and dining us.
   They wouldn't take no for an answer. We were forced to drink
   their sweet wine *straight*
(making a face)
                      out of gold and crystal goblets.

DIKAIOPOLIS
   Oh, city of the Acropolis, the arrogance of these envoys.

AMBASSADOR
   Among those barbarians, only the greatest gluttons
   and drunkards are called real men.

DIKAIOPOLIS
                          With us, it's the biggest   90
      lechers and whoremasters.

AMBASSADOR
                   In the fourth year, we reached
      the Great King's court. But he had already
      left with all his troops to take his ease
      in the Golden Hills.

DIKAIOPOLIS
                   And when, pray tell,
      did he come home again?

AMBASSADOR
                   At the full of the moon.
      He regaled us with pot-baked oxen.

DIKAIOPOLIS

> Pot-baked
> what? And how big were the pots?

AMBASSADOR

> He also served
> an enormous bird, three times as big as Kleonymus!

DIKAIOPOLIS

> The chicken general? Was the bird a rook? Like drachmas
> by rook or by crook?
> *(Enter Pseudobogus with two eunuchs.)*

AMBASSADOR

> I would like to present   100
> PSEUDOBOGUS, THE EYE OF THE GREAT KING!

DIKAIOPOLIS

> In a pig's eye you would! And may the Great Bird
> roost on your head and pluck out your eyes, Mister
> Ambassador.

HERALD

> THE EYE OF THE GREAT KING!

DIKAIOPOLIS

> With an eye to the main chance.

AMBASSADOR

> Now, Pseudobogus,
> tell the Athenians what the Great King
> commissioned you to say.

PSEUDOBOGUS

> Ootay Ow-Blay
> Oke-Smay Up-Ay Eir-Thay Arse-Ay.

AMBASSADOR

                              Now do you
     understand?

DIKAIOPOLIS
                    No, by Apollo, I didn't quite   110
     catch it.

AMBASSADOR
               He says that the Great King is going
          To send us gold.
     (to Pseudobogus)
                         Speak up now, and tell them
          clearly about the gold.

PSEUDOBOGUS
                         E-Thay Eat-Gray Ing-Kay
          Ill-Way End-Say Em-Thay Ool's-Fay Old-Gay.

DIKAIOPOLIS
     By Hades, I got that loud and clear!

AMBASSADOR
     What did he say?

DIKAIOPOLIS
                    He says that the Greeks don't
          have all their oars in the water if they think
          that the Persians are sending them gold.

AMBASSADOR
                              Not at all,
          He spoke of a load of gold.

DIKAIOPOLIS

A load, all right,
But not of gold. Now, get lost, I'll question   120
this bird myself.
(to Pseudobogus, showing his fist)
Now give it to me straight,
or this is for you, a knuckle kebab. Does the Great
King intend to send us gold?
(Pseudobogus shakes his head.)
The envoys
are giving us the shaft?
(Pseudobogus nods assent.)
These fellows nod
(indicating the two eunuchs attending Pseudobogus)
just like Greeks. In fact, I think they come from
around here. And this one is Kleisthenes,
the son of Sibertyius. Look how he's shaved
his hot little behind! So you've come to fake us
out, fake beard and all, as a eunuch,
you little monkey? And who's this other little shaver?   130
Can it be Straton, by any chance?

HERALD

Silence!
And take your seat. The Commission requests the Eye
of the Great King to dine with them in the Town
Hall.

DIKAIOPOLIS

Now wouldn't that drive you up the wall?
I get drafted and eat army rations, and these
phony rascals get royally entertained. All
doors are opened to them. Well, I've got news
for them that will make their hair stand on end!
Where is Amphitheus?

AMPHITHEUS *(reenters, glaring at the court officers)*
>   I'm right here.

DIKAIOPOLIS
>   Here, take these eight drachmas, go and make private   140
>   peace with Sparta for me, my wife, and children.
>   And not for anyone else.
> *(Amphitheus takes the drachmas and leaves. Dikaiopolis turns to the*
> *Commissioners and citizens.)*
>   And you're welcome
>   to get taken in by these Road Scholars!

HERALD
>   THEORUS, ENVOY TO THE COURT OF THRACE!

THEORUS *(entering)*
>   Here!

DIKAIOPOLIS
>   Another phony, about to be introduced.

THEORUS
>   Sirs, we would not have stayed in Thrace so long . . .

DIKAIOPOLIS
>   If it wasn't for the drachmas you were getting.

THEORUS
>   If it hadn't been for blizzards that covered Thrace
>   with snow and froze all the rivers, about
>   the time that Theognis was playing here. And all   150
>   that time, I was trying to hold up
>   my end, drinking with the king, Pitalkes.
>   What a lover of Athenians he is!
>   He even scrawls "The beautiful Athenians"
>   on his walls. And his son, dear boy,

is our very newest Athenian. He can hardly wait
to come here to the Festival and
eat our sausages. He begged his father to send
us aid with such an army that would make
everyone exclaim, "What a swarm of locusts   160
comes our way!"

DIKAIOPOLIS

                    That last is the only true
statement that you made.

THEORUS

                        He has sent you
the fiercest tribe in Thrace.

DIKAIOPOLIS

                      And here's the proof.

HERALD

THE THRACIANS UNDER THEORUS, COME FORTH!
(Thracian troops enter.)

DIKAIOPOLIS

What are they up to now?

THEORUS

                   THE GRAND ARMY
OF ODOMANTIA!

DIKAIOPOLIS

                 What kind of Odomantians
are gotten up like this?

THEORUS

                 Give them just two
drachmas wages a day and these archers
will overrun all of Boeotia!

DIKAIOPOLIS
>   Two drachmas for these circumcised barbarians?   170
>   The Athenian boatmen who are our first line
>   of defense are going to groan when they hear this.
>   *(An Odomantian steals Dikaiopolis' garlic.)*
>   Oh, misery! Those Odomantians
>   have copped my garlic! Drop it! Put it down!

THEORUS *(rounding on Dikaiopolis)*
>   You villain! How dare you attack them when
>   they're getting primed for battle?

DIKAIOPOLIS *(to the Commissioners)*
>   Will you allow
>   barbarians to walk all over me
>   like this in my own country? I warn you not
>   to hold an Assembly about the Thracians' pay.
>   I'm telling you I just felt a drop of rain!   180

HERALD
>   The Thracians are dismissed. Return in two days.
>   The Assembly is adjourned!
>   *(Everyone leaves except Dikaiopolis.)*

DIKAIOPOLIS
>   The garlic's gone,
>   so my salad is ruined.
>   *(Amphitheus enters, running.)*
>   But here is Amphitheus
>   back from Sparta. Welcome, Amphitheus!

AMPHITHEUS *(panting)*
>   Not till I stop running! The Acharnians
>   are after me!

DIKAIOPOLIS
                    What do you mean?

AMPHITHEUS
    I was bringing the treaties back here when some
    old geezers got wind of it and smelled them out.
    They're Acharnians and veterans of Marathon,
    as tough as oak with hearts to match. All   190
    at once they began shouting, "You scum! How dare
    you bring treaties here when all our vineyards are chopped
    down."
                    They began to pick up stones then,
    and I took off with them whooping and hollering
    behind me.

DIKAIOPOLIS
                    And so let them holler.
    Did you bring the treaties?

AMPHITHEUS
                                Yes, I did.
    There are three samples. Here they are. With each
    one there is a libation. These are for five
    years. Take a taste.

DIKAIOPOLIS
                    Yuk! Pfooey!

AMPHITHEUS
    What's the matter?

DIKAIOPOLIS
                            They stink of tar and bilgewater.   200

AMPHITHEUS
    Try these. They're the ten-year samples.

DIKAIOPOLIS
These smell of embassies to allies who will leave you
in the lurch.

AMPHITHEUS
Here, then, try the treaties
for thirty years on both land and sea.

DIKAIOPOLIS
Ah, now these are for a Feast to Dionysus!
They smell of nectar and ambrosia. And they don't
taste like army rations! I'll pour them out
and drink them down. And I couldn't care less
about the Acharnians. I am free of war
and free to hold a country Feast to Dionysus!   210
(Dikaiopolis exits into his house.)

AMPHITHEUS
And I'm getting out of here, away from those crazy
Acharnians.
(Amphitheus exits, as Chorus and citizens enter.)

CHORUS OF ACHARNIAN ELDERS
This way, everyone!
And ask whomever you meet which way that rascal
went. For the city's honor! Where did the man
with the treaties take himself off to?
He vanished into thin air. When Lacrateides
was in his prime, you can bet that fellow
would not have got off so easily. Why, I
could keep pace with *Olympians*. Did I ever tell you
I once placed second to Phaylius? And that   220
was with a load of charcoal on my back.
Oh, my joints are stiff and my legs are all shot,
but we'll catch the villain yet. He won't escape
the Acharnians. O Father Zeus, and all

the gods of heaven, who has dared to make peace
and lift up my enemies? I shall fight them
to the death to avenge my ruined vineyards
and never stop until I pierce them through
like a spiky reed. They will learn not to tread
my vines down. And we'll hunt that fellow from land   230
to land until he is found. And I'll not get
my fill of stoning him!

DIKAIOPOLIS *(from within his house)*
                         Keep silence! Keep holy silence.

CHORUS
    Be quiet, everyone! Did you hear his solemn
    call for silence? This is the man we are looking
    for. Now stand back, everyone. He's about
    to come out.

DIKAIOPOLIS *(entering, followed by his wife and daughter and two servants)*
                     Keep silence, holy silence!
(to his daughter and a slave)
    Now, Basket-bearer, you come out in front.
    And Xanthias, hold the phallus-pole up straight.

WIFE
    You may put the basket down, now, Daughter,
    and we'll begin the sacrifice.

DAUGHTER
                    Mother,   240
    pass me the ladle, so I can pour pudding over
    the cake.

DIKAIOPOLIS
        It goes well. O Dionysus, Lord
    and Master, look with favor on this solemn
    procession and sacrifice by me and my family,

in celebration of your rural feast,
and bring good luck to our peace of thirty years.

WIFE

Come, bear the basket prettily,
my sweet, and look demure. Lucky the fellow
who gets you and squeezes you so hard
that you break wind like a weasel! Go on now,   250
and make sure that no one steals your golden trinkets.

DIKAIOPOLIS

Xanthias, stay behind the basket-bearer.
You two fellows hold the phallus-pole
up straight, and I'll bring up the rear and sing
the phallic hymn. Wife, you watch
us from the roof. Forward!
(Wife, daughter, and servants exit. Dikaiopolis sings.)
O Phales, boon companion of Bacchus,
midnight rambler and carouser,
adulterer and lover, after
six long years of strife, welcome   260
to my home and house. I've made
a separate peace for myself.
So goodbye to fights and feuds and fusses,
and good riddance, General Lamachuses.
O Phales, how much sweeter it is
to catch a pretty thieving maid
and lie in a soft inviting glade
and make her pay a fine of kisses.
Come have a drink with me on the morning after,
and we'll drink a toast to peace, Phales, Phales;   270
hang our shields above the hearth forever after.

CHORUS

There he is, that villain who made peace
with our enemies! Stone him! Stone him!
Stone him harder, harder. Do him in!
(Acharnians throw stones at Dikaiopolis.)

DIKAIOPOLIS
> By Heracles! What's the matter with these madmen?
> You're going to smash my pot!

CHORUS
>   We're going to smash
> your *head*, you rascal!

DIKAIOPOLIS
>   O worthy Acharnians,
> why are you doing this?

CHORUS
>   You've got the gall
> to ask, you shameless shit? You filthy traitor
> to your Fatherland. *You* have the right   280
> to make treaties for yourself alone?
> How do you dare to look me in the face?

DIKAIOPOLIS
> But you don't know the reasons I made peace.
> Just listen to me!

CHORUS *(letting fly more stones)*
>   Listen to you? *You*
> are dead. We're going to bury you with stones.

DIKAIOPOLIS
> But you can't do that until you've heard my story.
> Hold on a minute, sirs!

CHORUS
>   There's no reason
> to delay. There's nothing to argue about,
> because we hate your guts even more than we hate
> Cleon's, and we're going to use his skin for shoes. 290
> So what do you think we're going to do to *you*?

We don't want to hear any pretty speeches from you,
the one who gave aid and comfort to the Spartans.
You're going to get what's coming to you.

DIKAIOPOLIS
Forget about the Spartans for a moment. Was I
right to make the treaty?

CHORUS
                              Right to make it?
No pledge is ever sacred to the Spartans,
even if you make it at the altar.

DIKAIOPOLIS
Still, I know that the Spartans, whom we hate,
weren't always entirely in the wrong and we   300
weren't always entirely right.

CHORUS
                              Not entirely,
you shameless rogue? You dare say this in public?
And that I should spare a traitor?

DIKAIOPOLIS
                              Not entirely,
not entirely! And I can prove how, often-
times, the Spartans suffered at our hands.

CHORUS
This terrible affair really vexes the heart
when you make bold to plead our enemies' case.

DIKAIOPOLIS
Yes, and if I don't plead it well and truly,
and the people show any doubt, I'm willing to lay
my head on the chopping block.   310

CHORUS
                              Why are you pulling back,
        fellow citizens? Let's tear him to pieces
        and dye his coat purple.

DIKAIOPOLIS
                         What black thoughts
        pervade your minds? Won't you hear me,
        Worthy Acharnians? Won't you hear me?

CHORUS
        For sure, I will not hear you.

DIKAIOPOLIS
                              I cannot bear
        the thought.

CHORUS
               I'll just be damned if I will.

DIKAIOPOLIS
        No one, Acharnians?

CHORUS
                         You have
        to die at once!

DIKAIOPOLIS
                    Then I'll make you suffer too!
        I have a hostage here that's very dear to you,
        and I'm going to bring him out and kill him, so   320
        that you can see your darling die.

CHORUS
                              Oh,
        fellow citizens, what can this mean

for us Acharnians? Can this man
actually hold a child of mine captive?
How can he be so bold?

DIKAIOPOLIS

                        All right, go ahead
and stone me.
(producing a coal scuttle from under his robe)
                    Here's the hostage, and I'm going to kill
him without mercy. We'll soon find out how much
you truly care for charcoal.

CHORUS

                    Then I'm destroyed,
it's a coal scuttle and truly a fellow citizen.
You cannot do what—you propose, sir. Never,   330
never!

DIKAIOPOLIS

            Go on, then, weep and wail. I'm putting
him to death, and I'll neither hear
nor heed you.

CHORUS

                If you do this, then you kill me.
I love charcoal with all my soul and we two
are of an age.

DIKAIOPOLIS

                Yes, but when I asked for
a hearing, I got none. You wouldn't even
hear me plead.

CHORUS

                Ah, but now it's different.
Now you may say anything your heart

desires. Even that you love our hated
enemies. I shall never be untrue   340
to this scuttle that I love.

DIKAIOPOLIS

All right,
then throw out all the stones you gathered on
the ground.

CHORUS *(dropping all their stones)*

Out they go, all of them.
But kindly put aside your sword.

DIKAIOPOLIS

But
I fear that you have other weapons hidden
in your clothes.

CHORUS

They're all gone, all
of them. See, I'm shaking out my robe.
Now put your sword away as you promised.
Look how I'm turning my clothes
inside out.

DIKAIOPOLIS

Yes, you should shake and shout   350
and send up your cries to heaven, while this poor scuttle,
in its fright, shook its dust all over
me, slain by the madness of its fellow
citizens! What a shame it is that men
have hearts as sour as unripe grapes, ever
ready to set up a roar and pelt stones
rather than hear a reasoned argument.
Even though I was willing to lay my head
on the chopping block to have my say about
the Spartans, make no mistake, I love my life.   360

CHORUS
>Oh, why don't you bring the block out right away.
>And give us the great oration you think will win
>us over. I'll be *delighted* to listen to it.
>Bring the chopping block out and start your speech.

DIKAIOPOLIS *(exiting into his house and returning with a chopping block)*
>All right, then here it is.

(aside)

>   And, even though
>I haven't got a friend, I'm going to speak
>my mind about the Spartans. Yet I'm afraid.
>I know the moods of country folk and how
>they love to hear some oily rascal cover
>them with praise: "My country, right or wrong!"   370
>They never dream they're being taken for
>a ride. Well do I know the minds of these
>old codgers. They like nothing better than a juicy
>trial and a verdict to sink their teeth into.
>I remember what I went through myself at Cleon's
>hands for last year's comedy, how he haled
>me into court and ranted and roared. He slanged
>and slandered me and slung mud till I
>was covered from head to foot.

(to the Chorus)

>   Permit me, then,
>before I start, to clothe myself as lowly   380
>and raggedly as I can.

CHORUS
>   Don't keep stalling.
>We won't stand for any more delay.

DIKAIOPOLIS
>Hold on a minute. I'm off to find
>Euripides.

(knocking on Euripides' door)

>   Ho, there! Boy!

CEPHISOPON *(opening door)*
Is someone
calling me?

DIKAIOPOLIS
Is Euripides at home?

CEPHISOPON
He is and he isn't.

DIKAIOPOLIS
He is and he isn't?

CEPHISOPON
He is
above, writing a play, but his mind
is absent, dreaming up verses.

DIKAIOPOLIS
O thrice-blessed
Euripides! Even his servant composes
witty dialogue. But call him anyway.   390

CEPHISOPON
It can't be done.

DIKAIOPOLIS
Nevertheless, I
won't go away. I'll pound on the door.
(pounding on door)
Listen
to me now, Euripides, Sweetheart!
It's I, Dikaiopolis!
(Cephisopon goes into house.)

EURIPIDES *(from within his house)*
I have no time!

DIKAIOPOLIS
  Wheel yourself out on stage.

EURIPIDES
                    It can't be done.

DIKAIOPOLIS
  Still?

EURIPIDES *(appearing at upstairs window)*
      All right, then, I'll appear,
  but I can't come down.

DIKAIOPOLIS
                    Euripides?
  Why do you write up there? Why don't you
  come down here? No wonder your heroes are all
  lame. They fall from a height! And why are you wearing   400
  such raggedy clothes? You look as if you're begging
  for alms! Now, will you lend me some of your rags
  from that old play of yours? What was the name of it?
  I have to address the Chorus today with a long
  speech, and if I don't impress them, it's curtains
  for me.

EURIPIDES
      Rags, rags? What are you talking
  about? Do you mean the rags Aeneas wore?

DIKAIOPOLIS
  Not Aeneas, no. Even scruffier
  than that.

EURIPIDES
      Those that blind Phoenix wore?

DIKAIOPOLIS
Not Phoenix. Even grungier.

EURIPIDES
You   410
must mean the tatters of Philoctetes, the beggar?

DIKAIOPOLIS
No, worse still.

EURIPIDES
Then how about
the disgusting rags of lame Bellerophon?

DIKAIOPOLIS
Bellerophon? But my fellow also limped
and begged. That fellow could talk a bird out
out of a tree.

EURIPIDES
Then you must mean Telephus.

DIKAIOPOLIS
The very same! Will you lend me some of his clothes?

EURIPIDES *(calling to Cephisopon)*
Boy! Fetch the rags that Telephus wore.
They're right above Thyestes' and mixed up with Ino's.

CEPHISOPON *(appearing at door, extending a ragged cloak on a stick)*
Here it is. It's all yours.
(Exits.)

DIKAIOPOLIS *(holding the tattered garment up to the light)*
Lord Zeus,   420
whose eyes can penetrate everywhere, let me be dressed

as loathsomely as possible. Euripides,
you've given me rags, now give me the cap to go with them.
Today, I have to act the beggar; to be
myself and yet not seem to be. The audience
will know me, but the Chorus will stand there gaping
like imbeciles, while I bamboozle them
with oratory.

EURIPIDES *(tossing a filthy cap down to Dikaiopolis)*
               Here, you're concocting tricky schemes.

DIKAIOPOLIS *(putting on the robe and cap)*
    And my best to you. I feel like Telephus already!
    But I need a beggar's staff.

EURIPIDES *(throws staff down to Dikaiopolis)*
                    Take it and leave my house.   430

DIKAIOPOLIS
    O my soul, look how I'm being thrown
    out, still needing so many articles.
    Euripides, give me a little round basket
    with a lamp inside.

EURIPIDES
               What on earth
    Do you need it for, you wretched fellow?

DIKAIOPOLIS
    It's not that I need it. I just want it.

EURIPIDES *(drops a basket and lamp to Dikaiopolis)*
    Now get out of here!

DIKAIOPOLIS
                May the blessing of heaven descend
    on you as it did on your mother.

EURIPIDES
                            Leave me in peace!

DIKAIOPOLIS
    Just one thing more. Give me a small cup
    with a broken rim.

EURIPIDES *(drops a cup to Dikaiopolis)*
                    Here it is. Begone!   440

DIKAIOPOLIS
    I'm going, but there's one tiny thing more, my dear
    sweet Euripides. A little pot
    with a sponge for a stopper.

EURIPIDES *(dropping a pot to Dikaiopolis)*
                            You're robbing me
    of a whole tragedy! Get out!

DIKAIOPOLIS
                        I'm going,
    I'm going now, but I have to have something else.
    If I don't get it, I'm done for. Sweetest, finest
    Euripides, I'll go after this and never
    darken your door again. Just give me some withered
    leaves to fill my basket.

EURIPIDES
                    You're killing me!
    My plays are disappearing right before my eyes.   450

DIKAIOPOLIS
    But enough, I'm going. I'm too importunate.
    No wonder the Powers That Be all hate me!
    But wait, I completely forgot the thing I need
    the most of all to succeed. My own sweet
    Euripides, may Hades swallow me up if I ask

for another thing. Give me a bit of chervil
like your mother used to sell?

EURIPIDES

The man's too insulting.
Close the doors of the house!
*(Euripides shakes his fist and withdraws. Cephisopon opens the door and
then slams it in Dikaiopolis' face.)*

DIKAIOPOLIS *(approaching the chopping block)*
My soul, now
we must go without the chervil.
(addressing the Chorus)

Are you aware
of the perilous battle we are about to engage in   460
by defending the Spartans? But now that we're fully steeped
in Euripides, take heart and toe the mark!

CHORUS

All right, now, what are you going to say and do?
Are you really shameless enough to debate us all?
Will you risk your neck and attack the State? *You*
were the one who asked for it. Now speak!

DIKAIOPOLIS

All of you who are watching, do not hold
it against me that I, a mere beggar, should dare
to address the Athenian people in a comic
play. For even comedy can discern truth.   470
I may say some things that startle you, but this year
Cleon cannot slander me by claiming that I
defame the State with strangers present. This
is the Lenaean Festival and no strangers are present.
We citizens are quite alone here now.
Make no mistake, I too am filled with hatred
for the Spartans. May Poseidon, Lord of Earthquakes,

bring all their houses down around their ears.
Because I, like you, have had my vines cut down.
But after all—and we are all friends here 480
today—how can we blame the Spartans for this?
It was some of our own people and not the State—
remember that I say it was *not* the State—
but some of our own, a few wicked little men,
worthless fellows with no scruples and less character,
who began spreading rumors that the Megarans
were importing contraband produce to the City.
Before long, not so much as a cucumber or a rabbit,
a suckling pig or a bit of garlic or salt
could come in without it being whispered that 490
it was Megaran and then promptly confiscated.
But the real trouble began when a few tipsy
young men went over to Megara one night
and kidnaped the courtesan, Simaetha. The Megarans
were cut to the quick and, in return, stole
two girls from the house of Aspasia. So all
of Greece went to war over three whores.
As we all know, Aspasia has Friends in High
Places. Pericles, from on high in Olympus,
unlimbered his heavy missiles. He thundered and lightened, 500
and befuddled all of Hellas. He enacted laws.
As the drinking song goes: "The Megarans presently depart
from earth and sea, from mainland and the mart."
The Megarans, dying of hunger, beseeched their Spartan
friends to get the Law of the Three Whores
rendered null and void. When the Spartans failed,
the instant clash of shields was heard.
                              But who
among us can say that they were in the wrong?
Do you mean to say that if the Spartans had stolen
so much as a small dog from one of our islands 510
we would have stood aside and said, "Be
our guests!" No, by heaven., we would have launched

three hundred ships of war, and the whole City
would have been infested with brawling troops and uproar
over the election of a Trierarch, the distribution of pay,
the gilding of figureheads, and the measurement of rations.
The navy dockyard would have rung with the sounds
of ships being built, of boatswains' pipes and flutes,
trills and whistles. Oh, yes, we would have done all
these things.
(shaking the beggar's staff)

> Even the beggar, Telephus, thinks so.   520
Anyone who doesn't is witless.
(The Chorus divides into opposing camps.)

SEMICHORUS I

> So *you* say,
you traitorous rascal! Do you dare to blame us
because we have informers? They are *our* informers.
Do we have to take this from a beggar?

SEMICHORUS II

> Well, by Poseidon,
he didn't lie. Every word he said was true!

SEMICHORUS I

True or untrue, is *he* the one to say it?
Just let me get my hands on him and I'll give him his due!

SEMICHORUS II

If you hurt him, you'll have to deal with me!
(They scuffle and Semichorus I is worsted.)

SEMICHORUS I

Lamachus, help! With your lightning glances
and terrifying aspect, kinsman and friend, come   530
in all your pride and glory. Can any leader,
any stormer of cities, compare to you?
Help me! Come quickly!

LAMACHUS *(entering)*
Where did that battle cry come from?
Where should I charge? Who has aroused the Gorgon
sleeping in my shield?

DIKAIOPOLIS *(in mock terror)*
O heroic
Lamachus, your plumes alone strike terror in
my heart.

SEMICHORUS I *(pointing at Dikaiopolis)*
O Lamachus, this man has been hurling
abuse at the State.

LAMACHUS
You, a beggar, dare
to say such things?

DIKAIOPOLIS
O Lamachus, forgive me
if I babble.

LAMACHUS
What was it that you said?   540

DIKAIOPOLIS *(stuttering)*
I can't remember. I'm so terrified of that Gorgon
on your shield . . . I beg you to put it aside.

LAMACHUS *(setting aside his shield)*
There, then.

DIKAIOPOLIS
Now turn it upside down so I can't see it.

LAMACHUS *(turning the shield upside down)*
Very well.

DIKAIOPOLIS
    Now give me a feather from your crest.

LAMACHUS *(handing him the feather)*
    Here, take the feather.

DIKAIOPOLIS *(using the feather to tickle the back of his throat)*
                    Now, hold my head
    while I puke. The crest turns my stomach.

LAMACHUS
    What? You use my feather to make you vomit?

DIKAIOPOLIS
    Is it really a feather, Lamachus? What kind
    of a bird did it come from? Was it from
    one of those big Bullshit Birds?

LAMACHUS
                    I'll kill you!   550

DIKAIOPOLIS
    Oh surely, Lamachus, that's not what mighty strength
    like yours is for. But if you're strong enough,
    why don't you circumcise me? Is that what your sword
    is for?

LAMACHUS
        A beggar like you dares to address a General like this?

DIKAIOPOLIS
    Am I a beggar, Lamachus?

LAMACHUS
                    What else?

DIKAIOPOLIS
    I am a good citizen and I'm not an ass-kisser.
    I've been on active duty here since the war
    began. You draw good pay. Can you say the same?

LAMACHUS
    The people elected me.

DIKAIOPOLIS
                        Three brain-dead
    nincompoops did, you mean. Ah, but that's   560
    what I despise. That's the reason why
    I made my treaty. There are gray-haired veterans
    on active duty in the lines while able-bodied
    young *gentlemen* like you are off somewhere
    in Thrace or Ecbatana, getting three drachmas
    a day—war heroes all—with battle scars
    from every dive and whorehouse from here to Babylonia.

LAMACHUS
    We were elected . . .

DIKAIOPOLIS
                        Sure you were. But how is it
    you young *gentlemen* always get paid, while these
    men
(pointing to the men in the Chorus)
            never do? Marilides, when have you ever   570
    served as an envoy? NEVER? And you, Trinides,
    Euphorides, Dracyllus, have you ever seen
    Ecbatana? Oh, no, these jobs are reserved
    for fine young *gentlemen* who never pay their bills,
    whom even their friends avoid like garbage
    thrown out through a window.

LAMACHUS
                        O Democracy, can I bear this?

DIKAIOPOLIS
> Not unless you get your pay, Lamachus.

LAMACHUS
> But I shall always wage war against
> the Peloponnesian people, harass them in every
> way I can, by land or sea and with all   580
> my might and main.
(*Exit.*)

DIKAIOPOLIS (*calling after him*)
> And I give full permission
> to all the Peloponnesian people to trade
> with me, but not with you, Lamachus.

CHORUS
> This man has won the war of words, and he
> has won over the people to his side
> about the truce.
> But it is time now
> to get ready for our anapests. Ever
> since our poet first began presenting
> his comic plays, he has never pushed himself
> forward or paraded his cleverness and wit.   590
> But now, because he has been slandered by
> his enemies and the Athenians are so quick
> to agree with them that he has ridiculed
> the City and them, he wishes to answer to
> these charges and to their fickleness.
> The poet says that he has done them a favor
> by daring to point out their errors to them,
> that if they are less likely now to be hoodwinked
> by cozening strangers and duped by flattering lies,
> they have him to thank for it. Always before,   600
> when foreign ambassadors wished to deceive you,
> they only had to call you the City of the Violet Crown.

DIKAIOPOLIS
>   At the word "violet," you'd sit bolt upright
>   on the beam ends of your bum and give them whatever
>   they wanted. Or, if they wanted to tickle your vanity,
>   they called you Shining Athens, Sleek Athens,
>   words better used to describe oily sardines.
>   For the poet's great service, then, you
>   should consider him a public benefactor
>   who has made you realize what democracy is all   610
>   about. And when strangers come to pay you tribute,
>   they wish to catch sight of this great poet,
>   who has dared to tell the truth. "Happy the city,"
>   the Great King said, "that heeds his wisdom. They will grow
>   and prosper, and triumph will be theirs." Thus,
>   when the Spartans offer you peace, if you will only
>   cede the isle of Aegina, it isn't the island
>   they want, it's the homeland of the poet. Take care
>   that you never lose him! He will always fight for what's best.
>
>   And so I say to all of you today,   620
>   let Cleon try his schemes and tricky ways,
>   I'll fight for what is right and just and true
>   and never be afraid and lie to you.
>
>   Come, O Acharnian Muse, with your fiery temper,
>   fierce and ardent, like a spark that leaps up
>   from coals of evergreen oak when it is fanned
>   by the bellows, as the small fish for frying lie ready
>   to hand and one person stirs the Thasian pickle,
>   and another dips the little fish in it.
>   Come to your countryman now with rough, rustic   630
>   song that is rousing and strong.
>   We graybeard veterans
>   wish to reproach the City, because it is not
>   right that we who fought great sea battles
>   in your service should not be cared for in our
>   old age. On the contrary, we

are cast aside and destitute, beset
by lawsuits brought against us by young orators
who sneer at our infirmities and flaunt
their legal skills. We are passed over now
and stand mute before our accusers, unable   640
to speak. Poseidon cannot protect us here.
Our only support is the stick we lean upon.
So we stand there in court, stammering and in
a fog, understanding nothing except that darkness
surrounds us. And the young accuser pounces upon
us with a barrage of legalese and sly
insinuations. He blinds us with rhetoric.
And poor old Tithonus stands there blinking and tongue-tied
as he is condemned and fined. And while he is leaving
he complains tearfully to a friend that the little   650
he had saved for a coffin was paid out now
in fines. What a scandal that veterans
with white hair who had saved the nation at Marathon
should now be reduced to penury by courts of law.
We who were pursuers on the field of battle
are now pursued in dotage, hunted down.
    What does the pettifogging lawyer say to this?
How pitiful it was to see Thucydides,
bent with age, browbeaten in court by the braggart
advocate Cephisodemus, the Scythian   660
as savage as the desert he was born in.
And I bled for the old man when he was beaten
by a court official. When he was in his prime,
he would have floored a dozen miserable
advocates and commanded an army of archers.
If you cannot leave us in peace, the least you can do
is to sort out the lawsuits and divide the writs
so that whoever sues the old and toothless
should be old and toothless too. Let the young sue
the young and hold the balance fair and square.   670

    (A change of scene to the Market of Dikaiopolis.)

DIKAIOPOLIS
> These are the boundaries of my marketplace.
> All of the Peloponnesians, Megarans, and Boeotians
> may trade here freely and sell to me, but not
> to Lamachus and he not to them. I appoint
> these three whips
(holds up three leather whips)
>   as market inspectors,
> and no stool pigeons will be allowed on these premises.
> I'm setting up a pillar here with a copy
> of my treaty on it for all to see.
(A Megaran enters with his young daughters.)

MEGARAN
> Hullo there, Athens Market that Megarans love!
> By Zeus, we have missed ye, as a mother does   680
> her kid. Come on, ye little darters of a poor
> unfortunate father. Try and find something to eat
> for yer old Dad. Now which would ye rather? To be sold
> or to go hungry?

DAUGHTERS
>   Oh, to be sold, to be sold!

MEGARAN
> I think so too, but who would be fool enough
> to buy ye? I know an old Megaran trick.
> I'll dress yez up as little porkers and put
> yez up for sale. Put these clogs on for trotters
> and no one will be the wiser ye're not blue-ribbon
> little sows. Now get in these sacks and make   690
> little pig-squealin' noises. Dikaiopolis!
> Ho, there! Are ye in the market for some tender
> little porkers in a poke?

DIKAIOPOLIS
>   Who are you?
> Are you from Megara?

MEGARAN

                    Yes, I've come to your agora,
for we've none in Megara.

DIKAIOPOLIS

                    How are things
In Megara?

MEGARAN

              Well, we have great hunger contests
as we sit around the fire.

DIKAIOPOLIS

                  Oh, it can be jolly
at the fireside if you have a piper.
What else is going on in Megara?

MEGARAN

                      The Council
is trying to decide how we can die the soonest   700
and get it over with.

DIKAIOPOLIS

                That's the best way,
get it all out of your system.

MEGARAN

    True.

DIKAIOPOLIS

    And what's the price of wheat in Megara?

MEGARAN

    Oh, it's priceless.

DIKAIOPOLIS

              And how about salt?

MEGARAN

We can't
get at it. It's controlled by the Athenians.

DIKAIOPOLIS

And garlic?

MEGARAN

Every time you raid us, you root
it all up!

DIKAIOPOLIS

What have you got to trade, then?

MEGARAN

These here little suckling porkers, the finest
in all of Meg'ra!

DIKAIOPOLIS *(looking into the sacks)*

Hm, they are, are they?
What kind of piggies are they?   710

MEGARAN

They're sows.

DIKAIOPOLIS

Oh, I don't think so.

MEGARAN

This is too much.
Do you disbelieve me?

DIKAIOPOLIS

They're sows of the human kind!

MEGARAN

No doubt, it's of my own breed. D'you want to hear
Them squeal?

DIKAIOPOLIS
Yes, I would.

MEGARAN
Squeal, little sowlet!
Squeal, or I'll take ye back home.

DAUGHTERS
Wee-wee, wee-wee, wee-wee.

MEGARAN
Now, are they little piglets or not?

DIKAIOPOLIS
It does seem so.
But let them grow up a bit and they'll be fine and fat.

MEGARAN
In five years, they'll be just like their mother.

DIKAIOPOLIS
But they can't be sacrificed, they're not perfect.   720
They have no tails.

MEGARAN
In time, they'll have fine long tails.

DIKAIOPOLIS
They're as alike as two peas.

MEGARAN
And from the same father
and mother. They'll be fine sows to offer Aphrodite!

DIKAIOPOLIS
But sows can't be offered to Aphrodite.
Can they eat without their mother yet?

MEGARAN

                         Sure,
and without their father, too.

DIKAIOPOLIS

                    What do they like
to eat?

MEGARAN

          Whatever you give 'em. Ask'm yourself.

DIKAIOPOLIS

    Do you like chick peas?

DAUGHTERS

                    Wee-wee, wee-wee, wee-wee!

DIKAIOPOLIS

    And how about figs?

DAUGHTERS

                    Wee-wee, wee-wee!

DIKAIOPOLIS

                         What fine squealing!
Someone, bring out some figs from the house!   730
(A servant appears with figs.)
    Look how they gobble the figs. I can't believe
they bolted them all down.

MEGARAN

                    Yes, they did,
except for the ones I took.

DIKAIOPOLIS

                    What funny creatures.
How much do you want for them?

MEGARAN

I think a bunch of garlic will be enough
for one and a quart of salt for the other.

DIKAIOPOLIS

Done,

and stick around awhile.

MEGARAN

I only wish
I could get as much for their mother.
(Informer enters.)

INFORMER

Ho there, fellow!
Who are you, and what are you doing here?

MEGARAN

I'm an honest pig merchant from Megara.   740

INFORMER

I'm going to denounce you and your pigs for what
you are, public enemies!

MEGARAN

Here
we go again. The *gonifs* are back.

INFORMER

Swear
at me in Megaran, will you? Let go of that sack!

MEGARAN

Dikaiopolis! Dikaiopolis! A rat
is in the marketplace and is turning me in!

DIKAIOPOLIS *(holding up the three whips)*
  Market inspectors, you're supposed to keep out
  that trash.

INFORMER
                But I'm denouncing our enemies.

DIKAIOPOLIS
  Get lost! And do your ratting somewhere
  else.
(He cracks a whip. The informer jumps and flees.)

MEGARAN
        They're like a pox on Athens.

DIKAIOPOLIS
                          Don't mind,   750
  Megaran. Here, take your garlic and salt
  that you bartered for. And fare well.

MEGARAN
                        We fare
  only ill in Megara.

DIKAIOPOLIS
                Let the wish
  apply to me, then.

MEGARAN
                    Farewell, my little sows,
  far from your father. May they give you salt
  for your bread here. May you munch it happily.
(Exit.)

CHORUS
  Here is a truly happy man, successful
  in everything he plans. He sits at home

in his own marketplace and makes a peaceful
living. Spies and lowlifes are not welcome   760
there, and you get true value for your wares.
(A Boeotian merchant enters, followed by Ismenas and a group of
musicians.)

BOEOTIAN
By Heracles, my shoulder aches.
(puts down a huge sack)
                                        Put
down the herbals over there, Ismenas.
And will you damned pipers pipe down!

DIKAIOPOLIS
Quiet, there! Get away from my door—
you musicians are worse than a swarm of hornets.

BOEOTIAN
Right you are, stranger. They've followed me
all the way from Thebes and blew all
the blossoms off my pennyroyal. I've got
everything for sale from chickens to locusts.   770

DIKAIOPOLIS
Hello, you muffin-eating Boeotian, what
have you there?

BOEOTIAN
                        Everything that's good
from Boeotia. I've got wicks for your lamp and mats
for your floor. I've got ducks and jays and waterfowl
and wrens . . .

DIKAIOPOLIS
                        You're bringing us fowl weather here,
Boeotian!

BOEOTIAN

           I've got foxes, otters, geese, and hens.
I've got eels from the lake. You just name it
and I've got it, friend!

DIKAIOPOLIS

                     Ah, your fish are
delicious. Let me taste your eels.

BOEOTIAN

                           Fifty
maidens I have here from Lake Kopais.   780
(addressing the eels)
        Come, complete the joy of our host!

DIKAIOPOLIS

        O my beloved! Too long lost, at last you're here.
May comic choirs sing thee to thy rest!
Ho, kitchen servants! Bring out the brazier
and the bellows. Just look at this darling eel,
after six long years away. Welcome her, children,
while I get charcoal, for this sweet stranger's sake.
May we never be separated again, even
in death. Take them in and cook them in beet leaves.
(Servants enter and take eels into the house.)

BOEOTIAN

        And what do I get in return?

DIKAIOPOLIS

                     This will pay   790
your market dues. Now, what else do you want
to sell me?

BOEOTIAN

           Why, everything.

DIKAIOPOLIS

                              For money or
for barter?

BOEOTIAN

        For Athenian wares that we don't have.

DIKAIOPOLIS

    For anchovies and pottery?

BOEOTIAN

                       We
have anchovies and pottery. I
want wares Boeotia doesn't have that you
have in plenty here.

DIKAIOPOLIS

                      Then I have just the thing!
Have you ever tasted pigeon, done to a crispy
turn? I'll pick up a stoolie for you, crate
him up for you.

BOEOTIAN

                   By the twin gods, I think   800
you've got it! I can make a fortune on him.
Take him from town to town and show him like
an ape.

DIKAIOPOLIS

        Just in time, here comes a pigeon
now, Nicharchus, coming to denounce you.
(Nicharchus enters.)

BOEOTIAN

    But look how small he is.

DIKAIOPOLIS

Yes, but it's all
pure spite.

NICHARCHUS

Whose merchandise is this?

BOEOTIAN

It's all mine, by Zeus. I brought it here
from Thebes.

NICHARCHUS

I hereby denounce it all. It's enemy
territory.

BOEOTIAN

You mean you've declared war on birds?

NICHARCHUS

On them and you, too.

BOEOTIAN

But what harm have I   810
done you?

NICHARCHUS

I will say this for whoever's standing
by. You are bringing a lantern wick here
from enemy territory.

DIKAIOPOLIS

You'd denounce him
for a lantern wick?

NICHARCHUS

That same lantern wick
could set fire to the docks.

DIKAIOPOLIS

And how could it do
that?

NICHARCHUS

If a Boeotian stuck it to a water
beetle and sent it, lighted, down a water-
way with a stiff breeze behind it straight
to the docks, our ships could be set ablaze and go up
in smoke.

DIKAIOPOLIS

Go up in smoke, you scoundrel, by a lantern   820
wick on a beetle's back?
(starts pummeling Nicharchus)

NICHARCHUS

I call the world
to witness this!

DIKAIOPOLIS

Gag him and bring me a litter.
I'll pack him up for shipment. This pigeon sings,
but he can't fly!
*(Servants enter with ropes and a litter; they tie Nicharchus up, then
leave.)*

CHORUS

Pigeon pie! Pigeon pie!
He can sing but he can't fly!
We say this for whoever's standing by!
(to the Boeotian)
You have a lovely package here. Be sure
and not to lose it.

BOEOTIAN

Yes, I'll be going now.
I'm just the boy to use it.

CHORUS

                       Farewell, worthy   830
stranger. Take this artful dodger and make
whatever good of him you can.

DIKAIOPOLIS

                       The rogue
was nothing but trouble. Boeotian, take him away!

BOEOTIAN

    Lift it up, Ismenas, and we'll be on our way.
(Boeotian and Ismenas exit, carrying Nicharchus.)

SERVANT OF LAMACHUS *(entering)*

    Dikaiopolis!

DIKAIOPOLIS

                What are you hollering about?

SERVANT

    Lamachus wants to observe the Dionysia.
He said to offer a drachma for some thrushes
and three drachmas for a Kopais eel.

DIKAIOPOLIS

    Lamachus. Who is that?

SERVANT

                   The terrifying
one, the awesome one who brandishes   840
the Gorgon shield and wears three dark plumes that shade
his helmet.

DIKAIOPOLIS

             An eel for *him*? Not if he gave me
his shield! Let him shake his plumes at his army rations.
If he doesn't like it, I'll call the market inspectors.
(Servant exits.)

As for myself, I'm taking all my goods home.
(sings)
> I'll fly away on thrushes' wings,
> and slip, slip like an eel away.

CHORUS
> Have you seen, all you people, how this prudent
> fellow who is infinitely clever,
> once he had made peace, may trade now every-   850
> where for useful household goods and things
> to eat that warm the heart. Whatever is good,
> it seems, is brought now to his door unbidden.

> But I shall never welcome Ares to my home
> or sing songs of battle in his company.
> Invite him to a peaceful home and he'll smash
> it up. He'll pull up vines and burn the poles
> that prop them up. He gets roaring drunk; he's not
> the one to drink a friendly loving cup.
> He's a basher and a mauler, a wrecker and a brawler.   860
> He likes nothing better than a tour of slaughter.

> But this man is proud of his good fortune
> and prepares a lavish banquet to show how well he lives.
> O Peace, sister of Aphrodite and the Graces,
> never before have I seen how sweet your face was.
> Would that Eros unite us in harmony,
> that Eros in pictures who wears a rosy crown.
> It may be I'm too old for you, but if
> I get you, there are three things that I may offer
> you: a long row of vines in perfect   870
> order; beside them tender cuttings of fig;
> and lastly a domestic vine, though I am old.
> Around them all, olive trees whose oil
> will anoint the two of us when the new moon shines.

HERALD *(entering)*

> Hear ye! Hear ye! As was the custom in days
> of yore, at the trumpet's call, drain your pitchers.
> And whoever sees the bottom first receives
> a wineskin as round as Ctesiphon's belly!

DIKAIOPOLIS

> Ladies and gentlemen, boys and girls, did you hear
> what the herald said? Quickly now, and turn   880
> the roasting meat on the fire. The rabbit is ready.
> Bring over the spits and I'll put the thrushes on them.

CHORUS

> How I envy you, you lucky man!

DIKAIOPOLIS

> And what
> will you say, when you see the thrushes roasting?

CHORUS

> I couldn't agree with you more!

DIKAIOPOLIS

> Stir up the fire, there!

CHORUS

> He knows so well how to cook a near perfect dinner.
> *(Enter an Athenian farmer.)*

FARMER

> Oh me! Oh me! Oh, woe is me!

DIKAIOPOLIS

> Heracles, who is there?

FARMER

> An unfortunate man!

DIKAIOPOLIS
    Then keep it to yourself!

FARMER
                    My dear friend,
    you are the only one who has a truce.   890
    Give me just a bit of it, even five years.

DIKAIOPOLIS
    What's your problem?

FARMER
                    I'm ruined! I lost my pair
    of oxen.

DIKAIOPOLIS
        How so?

FARMER
            The Boeotians stole them from Phyle.

DIKAIOPOLIS
    You are triply cursed! But why are you still wearing white?

FARMER
    Their dung allowed me to live in high luxury.

DIKAIOPOLIS
    So what do you want from me?

FARMER
                        I've lost my two eyes
    from weeping for my oxen. If you care
    for Dercetes of Phyle, rub some peace
    ointment on my eyes.

DIKAIOPOLIS
                    My dear fellow,
    I don't practice medicine.

FARMER
                                But please do,   900
    and I may find my oxen.

DIKAIOPOLIS
                        Impossible, go find
    a quack and whine to him.

FARMER
                            Just one little drop
    of peace. Pour it into this quill, please, sir.

DIKAIOPOLIS
    Not even a smidgen. Go and whine somewhere else!

FARMER
    My poor, poor oxen!
    (Exit.)

CHORUS
                        This man knows the joys of peace,
    and he's not about to share it.

DIKAIOPOLIS
                            Pour
    some honey over the tripe and start
    cooking the squid.

CHORUS
                    Do you hear his commanding voice?

DIKAIOPOLIS
    And be sure that the eel is browned.

CHORUS

                       Your words are driving
us mad with hunger as you speak.

DIKAIOPOLIS

                     Now roast   910
these other things and see that they're browned nicely.
(Enter a bridesmaid.)

BRIDESMAID

    A bridegroom is sending you this meat from his wedding
banquet.

DIKAIOPOLIS

       Very good of him, whoever he is.

BRIDESMAID

    And in return, he'd like to have you pour
him out a dram of peace into this pot
in order to keep him safely at home with his bride.

DIKAIOPOLIS

    Then take your meat away. I wouldn't give you
one drop of peace for ten thousand drachmas.
(Bridesmaid exits and then reenters.)
Now what is it this time?

BRIDESMAID

               A private message
from the bride.

DIKAIOPOLIS

         What does the bride want?   920
(Bridesmaid whispers something in his ear and he roars with laughter.)
Ye gods, what a ridiculous request.
She'll do anything to keep her husband's weapon

safely by her side. I'll do it! Bring me the truces.
She's only a woman, after all, and shouldn't
be made to bear the *privations* of war!
(to bridesmaid)

All right, now, girl, hold your medicine bottle
underneath the truces and tell the bride
to apply a drop of this where it is needed
most whenever they're drafting soldiers.
(Bridesmaid exits as servant enters.)

                                        Now, boy,

take the truces back and bring me a pitcher,   930
so that I can fill the winecups for the Feast.
(Servant leaves with truces and comes out again with pitcher.)

CHORUS

I see someone hurrying this way.
His brows are knitted like someone with a load of grief.

HERALD *(entering)*

O toils and broils and Lamachuses!

LAMACHUS *(entering)*

Who calls? Who makes a racket round my brassbound
halls?

HERALD

        The generals order you and your plumes
to lead your troops out to the snowy passes
to guard our borders. We've learned that a gang
of Boeotians plans to invade us during the Feast.

LAMACHUS

Ah, yes, the generals, there are so many   940
of them and they're worth so little. What
a shame it is that a man can't enjoy the Feast.

DIKAIOPOLIS

O gung-ho battle-ready host of Lamacheans!

LAMACHUS

Oh, no, not you again and your insults!

DIKAIOPOLIS

Do you dare to take me on, the four-winged Dragon?

LAMACHUS

Oh rats! What a load of grief that herald brought!

DIKAIOPOLIS

And this runner that I see, what tidings does he bring?

MESSENGER *(entering)*

Dikaiopolis!

DIKAIOPOLIS

Well?

MESSENGER

You must hurry
at once to supper. And be sure to bring your dinner
box and drinking cup. The High Priest   950
of Dionysus waits upon you. Supper
is ready. Everything is prepared: couches,
tables, rugs, wreaths, perfumes, sweetmeats,
courtesans, and there are meal cakes, flat cakes,
sesame and honey cakes, and lovely
dancing girls besides. So, come quickly!
(Exits.)

LAMACHUS

O wretched me.

DIKAIOPOLIS
> Don't complain, you picked
the Great Gorgon as your patron. Close up
your house and get your supper ready.
(During the next lines, boys come and go from Dikaiopolis' and
> *Lamachus' houses, carrying the various foods and*
> *objects they ask for.)*

LAMACHUS
> Boy! Boy! Bring me out my knapsack.   960

DIKAIOPOLIS
> Boy! Boy! Bring me out my dinner chest.

LAMACHUS
> Bring me the onions and salt with thyme.

DIKAIOPOLIS
> Bring me a piece of fish. I hate onions.

LAMACHUS
> Some pickled herring in a figleaf, boy!

DIKAIOPOLIS
> For me, some bacon on a leaf. I'll cook it here.

LAMACHUS
> Bring me the plumes for my helmet.

DIKAIOPOLIS
> And for me, my doves and thrushes.

LAMACHUS
> How beautiful and white this ostrich plume is.

DIKAIOPOLIS
> How golden brown this pigeon breast is.

LAMACHUS
>
> Man, stop ridiculing my armor.   970

DIKAIOPOLIS
>
> Man, stop leering at my pigeons.

LAMACHUS
>
> Bring me the case with the three crests on it.

DIKAIOPOLIS
>
> Bring me the basket with the hare's meat in it.

LAMACHUS
>
> Oh, the moths have eaten up my crests!

DIKAIOPOLIS
>
> I'm going to eat up this hare soup.

LAMACHUS
>
> Fellow, I'll thank you not to address me.

DIKAIOPOLIS
>
> I wasn't talking to you. The boy and I
> have made a bet. You decide, which
> is tastier, the locust or the thrush?

LAMACHUS
>
> You insolent cur!

DIKAIOPOLIS *(to the boy)*
>
> Locusts, he says, are much better.   980

LAMACHUS
>
> Boy, take down my spear and bring it here!

DIKAIOPOLIS
>
> Take off the sausage and bring it here!

LAMACHUS
>Hold the spear tight, I'll pull off the case.

DIKAIOPOLIS
>And, you, boy, hold the skewer tight.

LAMACHUS
>Boy, bring me the stand for my shield.

DIKAIOPOLIS
>And take the baked loaves out for me.

LAMACHUS
>Bring my round shield with the Gorgon on it.

DIKAIOPOLIS
>And bring me my round cheesecake, boy.

LAMACHUS
>This is out and out mockery, plain to see.

DIKAIOPOLIS
>This cheesecake is sweet, it's plain to see.   990

LAMACHUS
>Pour the oil out, boy. I see an old man
>reflected in it accused of cowardice.

DIKAIOPOLIS
>Pour out the honey, boy. In my cake
>I see an old man making a monkey of Lamachus.

LAMACHUS
>Bring out my breastplate armor, boy.

DIKAIOPOLIS
>Boy, bring out my winecup to warm my breast.

LAMACHUS *(putting on armor)*
    With this, I take up arms against the foe.

DIKAIOPOLIS *(lifting winecup)*
    With this, I can outdrink any man.

LAMACHUS
    Boy, lash the bedding to the shield.

DIKAIOPOLIS
    Boy, lash the supper to the chest.   1000

LAMACHUS
    I'll carry the knapsack myself, boy.

DIKAIOPOLIS
    I'll carry this meal and hurry off.

LAMACHUS
    Lift up the shield, boy, and be off.
    Ye gods, it's snowing. What a prospect!

DIKAIOPOLIS
    Pick up the dinner for the feast. Heavenly!
(Lamachus and Dikaiopolis leave separately with their servants.)

CHORUS
    Go now rejoicing on your separate ways,
    one to drink with laurels on his head
    and one to stand guard in the frozen wastes.
    One, lying with a sweet young beauty,
    is called to active duty in her bed.   1010

    A prayer

    May Zeus destroy the poetaster charlatan
    Historian Antimachus, the Spitter, Hocktoous,

who last year packed me off without my dinner.
May this curse befall the Director of the Chorus:
that as he reaches for a hot delicious seafood dinner,
a dog make off with it before he can begin it.
Next, as he is coming home one dark night,
may a footpad club him on the head.
May his hand reach out, as he gives chase,
and, for a rock, may he pick up a turd instead,   1020
and miss his aim and hit Cratinus in the face.

SERVANT *(entering and calling toward Lamachus' house)*
    Ho, you slaves in the house of Lamachus,
    heat up some water and bring it in a pot.
    Bring bandages and salve and greasy wool.
    In leaping over a ditch, the master wrenched his foot,
    and then he cracked his head upon a stone.
    The sleeping Gorgon on his shield came loose,
    and his Great Bird's plume fell in the mud.
    From prone on the rocks he raised this dolorous cry:
    "O illustrious sight, now I gaze   1030
    on thee for one last time. I leave
    the heavenly light. I am no more."
    He fell into the water and then jumped out
    to chase some robbers and prod them with his spear.
    But open up the doors, here he comes now.
(Servants come out from Lamachus' house. Reenter Lamachus, wounded,
         supported by attendants, and Dikaiopolis, jovial,
         crowned with bays, between two courtesans.)

LAMACHUS
    O woe is me! Woe is me!
    O vile misfortune! Chilling calamity!
    How I suffer, struck down by enemy spears.
    But even worse would be for Dikaiopolis
    to see me wounded and mock at my misfortune.   1040

DIKAIOPOLIS
Oh, bliss! What a day this is!
How firm and round their little tits are,
like quinces! What could be greater bliss, my treasures,
than your soft embraces and your golden kisses?
And at the feast, I was first to drain my winecup.

LAMACHUS
O wretched fate! O rotten luck!
Oh, oh, the painful wounds I suffer.

DIKAIOPOLIS
My dear Lamachippeus!
(kisses Lamachus)

LAMACHUS
                        What
an abomination!
(bites Dikaiopolis)

DIKAIOPOLIS
                Oh, great gods!

LAMACHUS
Why did you kiss me?

DIKAIOPOLIS
                    And why did you bite me?   1050

LAMACHUS
What a load of aggravation!

DIKAIOPOLIS
                    The Feast's
a time for celebration.

LAMACHUS

O Paean,
physician of the gods, heal me!

DIKAIOPOLIS

It's not
Paean's festival today.

LAMACHUS *(to servants)*

Lift me
gently, friends. Oh, how I suffer.

DIKAIOPOLIS *(to courtesans)*

Lend me a hand here for my middle member,
darlings, both of you.

LAMACHUS

The blow from the stone
has made me dizzy. Everything is dim.

DIKAIOPOLIS

I want to lie down, too, and screw until I'm dizzy.

LAMACHUS

Bear me gently to Pittalus' clinic.   1060

DIKAIOPOLIS

And take me to the judges of the feast,
because I've won the wineskin.

LAMACHUS

A lance has cut me to the bone. Oh, what a torture.
(He is carried off.)

DIKAIOPOLIS

Do you see my empty pitcher? Hail the conquering hero!

CHORUS

    Hail the conquering hero, as you say,
    O august one.

DIKAIOPOLIS

                 I took it straight and drank
    it chugalug.

CHORUS

             Hail triumphant, noble
    heart. Make way for the wineskin!

DIKAIOPOLIS

                   Follow me, all,
    and sing "Hail the conquering hero."

CHORUS

                  We'll follow
    you and your wineskin and sing it as we go.   1070
    Hail the conquering hero.

Peace

Translated by
Fred Beake

There are two sensible approaches to the translation of Aristophanes. One is to do as Alan Somerstein does in his fine translation of *Peace* in the Penguin Classics, and concentrate on rendering the humor per se. This means inevitably a text that is somewhat different from the Greek, because literal translation destroys such things as puns. The purpose of such a translation is to produce an accessible version for the late twentieth century, and this is a worthy aim. However, this process does tend to distance us from what Aristophanes actually wrote.

Aristophanes' Greek is not purely comic. In *Peace* much indeed is very serious, even when the seriousness is larded with humor. One thinks of the treatment of Trygaeus at the beginning of the play. Of course Trygaeus is mad, but because he is mad he can see the evil inherent in a war that the sane pretend in their conscious minds to accept. His solution is of course comic. To go to Heaven on a dung beetle is not the most rational of actions, but the effect is the end of a war. Similarly, the strange knock-about section with the false prophet Hierocles toward the end of the play is very ambiguous. Of course it is funny, and the warmonger Hierocles gets put down; but equally he says the things about war that Aristophanes must have known would not go away from the real world, however much he might desire it.

Similarly, for all the humor and the parody the essence of the great choruses of this play is deeply serious. It is typical indeed that at the end the Age of Iron is put by and we revert to an older pastoral civilization.

This theme is central to this very various play. The Spartan/Athenian War has caused the Attic country folk to take refuge in the City of Athens as protection against the annual Spartan raids. Here, out of their element, they have upset the balance of Athenian Democracy, have been used unscrupulously by various demagogues and by the enemies of Athens, and have ejected the goddess Peace. In the play at least the natural balance is restored. And in a way that is reminiscent of the 1960s (or perhaps the '20s) to anyone who lived through them, the message is "Make love not war." It is not for nothing that Madame Ambassador has "license for five years' fucking," or that she ends up offering her services in a public-spirited way.

I therefore wanted in my translation to keep as close as possible to the Greek, so as to convey the comedy and the seriousness of this complex, often ambiguous play. I wanted in particular not to sacrifice the sense of the original for the sake of recreating a pun, but instead to use any natural wordplay and puns I could discover in the composition of the English. Thus I introduce Ares' "sister in war," despite its strict absence in the Greek. This decision solved one problem but caused another, for the sense of some passages is odd to modern ears; whether it is any odder than, say, some passages of Shakespeare is a good question. I only altered the original where some explanation seemed totally unavoidable. Usually this took the form of a brief addition to the text. Thus, in the very difficult speech in which Hermes and the Chorus give us Aristophanes' view of recent Athenian history, it seemed reasonable to slip in that Pheidias is a sculptor. However, I have kept such insertions to a minimum.

It has become fashionable recently to say that Aristophanes was a prose writer manqué, who wrote in verse because he had to. I thought this idea dubious when I started the translation. Now I have finished it I am sure it is ridiculous. There is a gravity and a beauty to the Greek that is extraordinarily spontaneous, even when the most ludicrous things are happening on stage. Hierocles' false prophecies are meant to sound ridiculous, but equally there is something eerie and powerful about them. War is a comic figure, but he is also rather frightening.

I therefore concluded that the translation must be in verse, and since it is my own idiom I used free verse. This is rather formal in general, and with a touch of the older blank verse, during the opening scene by Trygaeus' house, and the second scene in Heaven in which Peace is rescued from War. However, I felt that something more irregular (and for sake of argument post-William Carlos Williams) was needed in the final scene after the return to Earth, both because this material seems less formal to a modern ear and because of a certain tentativeness in the Greek.

The original choruses, a producer should perhaps be reminded, used an element of dance, but we do not really know a lot about it. A modern producer might well introduce an element of voices moving in and out of a texture. I have made some modest proposals in that direction, but they could be expanded.

There are very few stage directions in the original. I have introduced some for the sake of clarity, but they can be ignored or reinvented at will. My directions assume a proscenium arch style of stage.

Finally, I must thank David R. Slavitt for commissioning what has been a most pleasurable task, and Cath Finch for much practical help.

Cast

TRYGAEUS
FIRST SERVANT
SECOND SERVANT
CHORUS of girls, ages 8–15
HERMES, messenger of the Gods
WAR
UNREST
CHORUS of characters from all Greece
CHORUS of farmers (male and female)
CHORUS leader/Aristophanes
HIEROCLES, a false prophet
SICKLE MAKER
CREST MAKER
BREASTPLATE SALESMAN
TRUMPETER
HELMET SALESMAN
SPEAR SALESMAN
TWO SMALL BOYS
NONSPEAKING
 Propman
 Opora
 Madame Ambassador
 Parliamentarian
 People with firewood
 Tradesmen
 People out of work

*(The time is during one of the periodic wars between Athens and
 Sparta. At left is the courtyard of the house of Trygaeus, an
 Athenian of some importance, now widely believed to be mad.
 At the right are a man, who will turn out to be Trygaeus, and an
 enormous mechanical beetle. The man is asleep. Two very dirty*

servants in rough attire are busy in the courtyard around a large pot. One is stirring it. The other keeps running in with a cake tin, which he fills with a very dubious mixture, and then takes to the beetle, who consumes it voraciously, leaving the servant to return with the empty tin for more.)

FIRST SERVANT

Bring, bring the barley cake—quick as you can, for Mr. Beetle.

SECOND SERVANT

Give it to him, the worst washed of all.

FIRST SERVANT

Here it is.

SECOND SERVANT

And may he never eat a barley cake as sweet.

FIRST SERVANT

Give him another, molded from what comes out of a donkey.

SECOND SERVANT

Here it is—the same again.

FIRST SERVANT

But where is the one that you just brought?
He has not eaten it!

SECOND SERVANT

No, by our Lord, but he snatched it up
and consumed it, having twiddled it about with his feet.   10

FIRST SERVANT
 Quickly, quickly, mix up lots and knead them well.

SECOND SERVANT *(addressing the audience)*
 Gentlemen scavengers, stand firm for me before the Gods
 if you do not wish me to choke as you watch.

FIRST SERVANT
 Give him another, give him another—it's a boy's best friend—
 and he says he wants it well pressed.

SECOND SERVANT
 But gents, for me there is one let out in this:
 there's no one to say that I nibbled the cake in the bowl.

FIRST SERVANT
 Oh well, bring another, another, and another,
 and quick, mix some more.

SECOND SERVANT
 No, by Apollo, not me. I can't: 20
 it's like as if the bilges are overflowing.
 But I will take it and chuck the lot.
(throws it over the audience)

FIRST SERVANT
 Ee, by Zeus, to the crows and you with it!

SECOND SERVANT *(to the audience)*
 Can any of you lot tell me
 where I can get a nose without a hole?
 For there's no more gruesome job
 than the kneading that's necessary
 to provide the beetle with its grub!
 A pig goes and shits (or a dog),
 and doesn't take that much notice.   30

But this arrogant sod gives himself a swagger
about it, says it's much too good to eat
unless I spend the whole day mashing it up
like a rich round cake for a lady's table.
But I'll look in and see if he's finished with his grub;
open the doors—just so, so he can't see me.
(aside)
Stuff away, and don't let anything stop your eating.
Just forget about yourself, and burst.
(to audience)
Oh, the sod! He eats, head in the trough,
setting his teeth in like a wrestler,   40
twisting his head this way, and his hands
that—like he was twisting
the cables for hauling barges.
Disgusting thing—evil smelling, can't stop eating.
What badge of what god he wears I don't know.
Can't be Aphrodite, or the Graces neither.

FIRST SERVANT
Then whose badge is it?

SECOND SERVANT
Suppose it must be the mark of Zeus Dung Gatherer.
Now I expect someone in the audience—
some young know-it-all—is muttering   50
"What's going on? What is the beetle?"
And some fellow with pretensions to philosophy
is sitting there saying, "I reckon
this is all about Cleon—this creature
who's so shameless about eating his own shit."
But I'll go and give the beetle his drink.

FIRST SERVANT
But me, I'll tell it to the boys
and the young men, and the not quite so young men,

and speak it to the men of importance,
and above all to the men of very great importance.   60
My master is mad in a new way.
You haven't seen this before; this one's quite new.
Every day he stares at heaven
and, mouth gaping, is reproachful to Zeus,
saying, "Lord, what is it you want to achieve?
Put down your broom. Cleanse Hellas no more."
*(On the other side of the stage Trygaeus wakens as if from some dreadful
nightmare.)*

TRYGAEUS
    Ah! Ah!

FIRST SERVANT
    Quiet! I think I hear his voice.
*(Trygaeus is in good quality clothes that were once new. He looks wild,
but not quite mad. He raises his hands to heaven.)*

TRYGAEUS
    Zeus, why do you do such things to your people?
    See yourself as you wrack the cities!   70

FIRST SERVANT
    There it is. There's that nonsense again I was talking of.
    That's the outline of his madness: listen to it.
    But this is what I heard him say
    when the fit first came upon him.
    He started talking to himself, and he said,
    "If I could come now to my god."
    And he got some long thin ladders made
    and tried for heaven;
    but it wasn't no use, and he cracked his head.
    Then day before this he slipped off I don't know where,   80
    and he brought back a great beetle from Aetna,
    and he got me to groom it like a horse,

and he spoke to it nicely like a young colt.
"Pegasus mine, of noble flight," says he,
"You must lift me straight to Zeus."
But now time to look in and see what he's up to.
(*The servant goes in to find that Trygaeus has saddled his beetle and
                    mounted it. As the servant enters, the beetle rises
                    above the house.*)
Dreadful thing! Here, everyone, here!
The master—he's mounted up on the beetle
like on a horse, and he's up in the air.

TRYGAEUS
    Quietly, quietly, with calm, my beast!   90
    Don't be too proud that you're carrying me,
    but from the beginning trust in your strength,
    even though the joints of your wings
    are not yet moist and easy.
    And breathe no evil upon me, I beseech you.
    And if you mean harm, why stay at home
    with all the things that are mine.

FIRST SERVANT
    Master, master, you are beside yourself.

TRYGAEUS
    Be quiet! Be quiet!

FIRST SERVANT
    But why are you talking such rubbish?   100

TRYGAEUS
    I fly for every Greek.
    I carefully prepare a new venture.

FIRST SERVANT
    Why cherish your fury? What is wrong with not being mad?

TRYGAEUS

    You must summon me words of good omen—not
    mutter nothings, but cry to Heaven in a joyful way.
    And all men must be directed to silence,
    and the sewer and the loo must be shut up with bricks,
    and constipation urged on all asses.

SECOND SERVANT

    Well, I'm not going to shut up, not unless
    you tell me where you're thinking of flying off to.   110

TRYGAEUS

    But where should I go—
    except to God and his heaven?

FIRST SERVANT

    Now, why have you got that in your head?

TRYGAEUS

    I mean to ask him about the Greeks—
    all of them—and what he means to do with them.

FIRST SERVANT

    And if he won't tell you?

TRYGAEUS

    Then I shall indict him—
    as the betrayer of Greece to the Medes.

FIRST SERVANT

    No, by Dionysus, not while I'm alive to stop it.

TRYGAEUS

    There is nothing except this.   120

FIRST SERVANT
>   Come, come, children. Your father
>   is going to steal off to Heaven
>   and abandon you to desolation.
>   Beseech your father, you girls that Fate has cursed.
> *(A Chorus of small girls in a state of agitation rushes on stage. They*
> *address their father in ascending order of age.)*

GIRL
>   Daddy, Daddy, what is the truth
>   about what is being said in the rooms of our house,
>   that you would go with the birds and leave me
>   and wander with crows alone?
>   What is the truth? Tell me Daddy, if you love me.

TRYGAEUS
>   It is as it appears, my little girl,   130
>   and in truth I am cross with you,
>   that you should come and ask me for bread,
>   and call me Daddy, when there is not any silver
>   at all within the house.
>   But if I should ever return successful,
>   why in no time there'll be buns
>   and a hot spanking sauce for you.

ANOTHER GIRL
>   But what are the means by which you shall go?
>   A ship is no use for this journey.

TRYGAEUS
>   I have a winged beast to bear me;   140
>   I shall not be on board ship.

ANOTHER GIRL
>   But what's the point of your harnessing
>   a beetle to reach the gods, dad?

TRYGAEUS

> In the words of Aesop it is found that this
> is the only winged creature to have attained to the gods.

GIRL

> What you're saying's pretty dubious, Daddy,
> that a smelly old beast reached the gods!

TRYGAEUS

> He came in his anger against the eagle long ago,
> and he hurled out the eggs in the magnificence of his revenge.

ANOTHER GIRL

> But shouldn't you have harnessed Pegasus and his wings   150
> and come in proper tragic fashion before the gods?

TRYGAEUS

> But it would have taken two lots of supplies,
> and this way I eat my fill,
> and from that we get his fodder.

ANOTHER GIRL

> And what if he should take a great dive
> into the waters of the sea? How could
> he get out with only his wings?

TRYGAEUS

> I've got a steering oar; I'm all ready for that.
> This boat is Naxos built and Beetle class.

ANOTHER GIRL

> And what shore shall receive you kindly in your wandering?   160

TRYGAEUS

> Well, Piraeus has got its Beetle Cove.

GIRL *(the eldest)*
> Beware, in case you slip and fall
> headlong, and lame provide Euripides
> with a plot, and become a tragedy.

TRYGAEUS
> I will be careful of that. But now goodbye!
> It is for you I do these deeds.
> Do not fart or shit for three days,
> or the scent will carry to the height, and he will
> turn his nostrils down and throw me off, and graze.

(The stage goes into darkness. Only the beetle is visible above it as it
carries Trygaeus through the stars of the sky. On
the stage the set of Heaven is being prepared.)

> But come, my Pegasus, be happy, be glad.   170
> Set your gold bridle to clink,
> and with ears bright, depart.
> Why do you do it? Why do you it? Why
> do you incline your nostrils to loos?
> Rise quickly from this earth
> and with swift wing outspread
> rise at once to the halls of God.
> Avert your nose from shit
> and all the days of fodder.
> Oh, man, what do you do, that you shit   180
> among the brothels of Piraeus?
> If you would undo me, undo me. If you would not
> hurl me down, lay all foul under earth
> and sow only thyme above, and pour out
> sweet scents. For if I should fall
> into evil plight, then for my death
> the citizens of the town of Chios
> will be forced to pay five talents,
> and all because of your ass.

(The beetle descends almost to head height. A propman rushes in front,
almost collides, and laughs in a grotesque way.)

You frightened me! I cannot see the joke.   190
Propman, keep your mind on me!
I've got the colic. There's wind in my gut.
You just watch out. I'll feed my beetle.
(The lights come up on a strange surreal landscape with a few rocks. A
strange figure, Hermes, is wandering about rather
indecisively outside the front of a house.)
But now I think I must be close to the gods.
I look down on the house of Zeus.
What is inside the doors of Zeus? Will you not open?
(The beetle lands, and then makes a very slow and awkward takeoff.)

HERMES
How did it get here—is it something human?
By Heracles, what is that awful thing?

TRYGAEUS
A horse-beetle.

HERMES
Unclean, foolhardy and shameful man,   200
unclean, very unclean, unbelievably unclean,
how did you come hither, uncleanest of unclean?
What is your name? Why do you not tell it me?

TRYGAEUS
The uncleanest.

HERMES
What is your country? Tell it me.

TRYGAEUS
The uncleanest.

HERMES
Who is your father?

TRYGAEUS
    What, mine? Oh, the uncleanest.

HERMES
    You'll be under the ground, if not dead,
    if you don't tell me your name, and summat about yourself.   210

TRYGAEUS
    I am Trygaeus from Athmona,
    my craft is the dressing of vines.
    I speak no slander, engage in no lawsuit.

HERMES
    But why have you come?

TRYGAEUS
    To bring burnt offerings for you.

HERMES
    And how did you come, you silly little man?

TRYGAEUS
    Well, you greedy pig, I see that in your sight
    I am no longer the uncleanest man about.
    Well, get on with it! Call Zeus for me.

HERMES
    Hang on, hang on, hang on: 220
    truth is you're nowhere near the gods.
    That lot packed up yesterday, and went.

TRYGAEUS
    Where on earth?

HERMES
    Oh, somewhere or other, you know.

TRYGAEUS
    But where?

HERMES
    Oh, a long way off—
    to the uttermost parts of the sky.

TRYGAEUS
    How come you were left here alone?

HERMES
    To keep an eye on what they left behind—
    their bits of crockery in the main.   230

TRYGAEUS
    Why ever did the gods depart?

HERMES
    Furious with the Greeks they were. And so,
    where they had been they got in Mr. War as tenant
    and handed over you lot to do as he thinks best.
    And they've set up house as high as they can get,
    so they don't have to watch your fights,
    or take any notice when you start your praying.

TRYGAEUS
    And why have they done such things to us? Tell me.

HERMES
    Because you asked for war
    when they labored all the time for peace. And if   240
    the Spartans got the upper hand a bit
    they'd talk like this:
    "By the twin god, now Athens shall yield the right."
    And if the Athenians had got the best of it
    and it was the Spartans that wanted peace,

you'd say at once: "We are being taken in.
They'll be here again while we have Pylos."

TRYGAEUS

That's certainly how the people in my country talked.

HERMES

But I do not know if what is left of Peace
will be seen again.   250

TRYGAEUS

But where's She gone?

HERMES

War chucked Her in a pit.

TRYGAEUS

Whereabouts?

HERMES *(indicates one of the clumps of stones)*
Right underneath that, and you can see
the size of the stones he put on top.

TRYGAEUS

Tell me,
what is he making ready to do to us?

HERMES

I don't know, 'cept this last evening
he brought along this huge, absolutely gigantic mixing bowl.

TRYGAEUS

What does he mean with this mixing bowl?   260

HERMES

He means to mash the cities in it.

But I'm off. He's coming out, judging by the
divine uproar. What a row in there!
(Hermes exits. Enter War from the house, dressed in leather with huge
boots. He carries a large mixing bowl. There are
loud sound effects as if of great boots, and
something scraping.)

TRYGAEUS
How wretched is my lot. Lead my feet
away from him.
(crouches behind some rocks)
I think I hear it—
mixing bowls wild with the warrior noise.

WAR
Hi man, hi man, hi man full of moans.
This'll bring some pain to your jaws.

TRYGAEUS
By Apollo, what a broad bowl!
And how evil the look of War!   270
Is this the he that we flee—
the terrible, the thick-skinned,
the one that stays on his feet?

WAR *(adding leeks)*
O you of Prasiae, three-fold and five-fold unfortunate
in multiples of ten, your end's today.

TRYGAEUS
All right, everyone: nothing to do with us.
It's bad, but it's for the Spartans.

WAR *(adding garlic)*
Megara, Megara, thou art handed over, wholly
and now to be salad.

TRYGAEUS

Gracious, goodness gracious—how big and sad   280
are the tears he's putting in for the Megarans.

WAR *(adding cheese)*

O Sicily, soon you will be gone!

TRYGAEUS

O sad cities to be so grated!

WAR

And now I add honey of Athens.

TRYGAEUS

Heh, I don't think you should add that:
it costs a bob. Watch it with Athenian honey!

WAR

Boy! Boy! Unrest!

UNREST *(entering)*

You want me?

WAR

You'll weep buckets.
What are you standing there for like an idiot?   290
Well, here's my fist.
(punches him)

UNREST

Such pain for me! How unfortunate I am! Mister,
you've gone and got garlic on your fist.

WAR

Run off and get a pestle.

UNREST

> But, my dear, we haven't got one:
> we only got here yesterday.

WAR

> So be quick and borrow one from the Athenians.

UNREST

> I'll go, by Zeus. Otherwise I'll have cause to moan.
> *(Exit.)*

TRYGAEUS

> Ah well, what may we do, we poor mortality?
> See the fist, huge above us.   300
> If he comes and brings the pestle,
> then War will sit and crush the cities,
> but, by the Lord of Misrule,
> may it be lost, and he not bring it back!
> *(Enter Unrest in a tizz.)*

UNREST

> Hi!

WAR

> So what is it? Why haven't you brought it?

UNREST

> You wouldn't believe it. It's lost—that Athenian pestle.
> It's that seller of leather—the one that stirred up Greece.

TRYGAEUS

> Oh marvelous, Athena, our lady, our mistress.
> He's lost it before the salad was mixed for us,   310
> and the State remains.

WAR
>Oh, skip off and get that other one from the Spartans.

UNREST
>Ok, Mister.
>
>*(Exit.)*

WAR *(to Unrest's back)*
>And come back quick.

TRYGAEUS
>Why are we so tested? Now is the summit of our crisis.
>If there is someone from Samothrace,
>a true initiate, now is the time for the perfection of prayer
>to mislead his foot on the way.
>
>*(Enter Unrest in an even worse tizz.)*

UNREST
>O me, I am sad. O me, O me, I am out of luck!

WAR
>Well, what is it? Why haven't you brought it me?   320

UNREST
>It is lost. The pestle
>of the Spartans is lost.

WAR
>How, you stupid ha'porth?

UNREST
>They lent it to friends in the land of the Thracians.
>And they lost it.

TRYGAEUS
>Good! Well done, you gods that are twin!
>It has come out well again. Rejoice, all men!

WAR

> Oh, pick up these little bits
> and take them off somewhere.
> Me, I'll be inside making myself a pestle.   330

(War goes into the house, followed by Unrest.)

TRYGAEUS

> Now is the time for the song of Datis,
> when he had grown mellow in the early afternoon.
> "I am happy, and gladly, and joyfully."
> Now, people of Greece, is our blessed time—
> release from toil and release from struggle,
> as Peace chases away all evil
> before another pestle can arise.
> But, farmer, merchant, joiner, smith,
> foreigner living here, and stranger passing through,
> and you men of the Islands,   340
> come hither all and leave your place,
> quick as you can, with crowbar and rope.
> For now the spirit of goodness is among us all.

(Enter a Chorus of numerous workmen with tools. They are sharply
divided, however, between farmers in smocks,
which are by no means clean, and townsmen in
much cleaner, less sensible clothes.)

CHORUS

> Come and dance with all your heart and at once for this
> deliverance!
> O, all you Greeks, we shall have the necessary help, now, if ever,
> we are delivered from the ranks of war and its bloody evil.
> And this day shall outshine abomination.
> And, whatever must be done to remedy our situation,
> tell me what is the problem, and it shall be undertaken.
> It seems to me that we must not end this day   350
> before with crane and crowbar we have dragged into the light
> She that is greatest of Gods, and loves the vine.

TRYGAEUS

Oh, will you not be quiet. Or do you want
the row of your celebration to enkindle War?

CHORUS

But we have heard your proclamation and rejoice,
for it was not, we note, "to depart with three days rations, and at
once."

TRYGAEUS

But you watch out for Cerberus in there,
in case he comes wheezing and croaking as before,
and we find there's a problem and the Goddess cannot be
extracted.

CHORUS

There is someone who would take Her as booty,   360
someone who would snatch Her from my arms! Oh! Oh!

TRYGAEUS

Chaps, you're going to ruin me if you don't stop your row.
He will sally out and crunch us with his feet!

CHORUS

Let him muddle all, trample all, and beat it down:
there is no stopping my delight this day.

TRYGAEUS

Why this nonsense? What's up? By the gods, do not let
this wonderful thing be spoiled by your prancing!

CHORUS

I really did not mean to dance.
My pleasure went beyond my intention
and my leg made a pattern.   370

TRYGAEUS

But that's enough, now, stop it, stop your dancing!

CHORUS

But see, I've stopped already.

TRYGAEUS

You say so, but you don't stop.

CHORUS

Just let me swing along a bit, and then I'll stop.

TRYGAEUS

Well, one more go, and then no more.

CHORUS

And then no more dancing, if it will help you.

TRYGAEUS

But look here, you haven't stopped.

CHORUS

Oh, just another twirl for Zeus
and then I'll stop my right leg.

TRYGAEUS

Oh, you can do that, and then no more tricks.   380

CHORUS

But the left leg's got to have its turn.
For I am happy, and rejoice, and am merry in my laughter,
not least because old men can at last put down their shields.

TRYGAEUS

Please don't rejoice now! The way ahead's not clear.
When we've got a firm hold on Her,

then will be time to rejoice,
to yell, to laugh.
And then you will be able
to sail, to be still, to move, to sleep,
to examine all the sights,   390
to feast, to try the latest games,
to enjoy life, to yell
to your heart's content.

CHORUS

Oh, may it happen that I see that day!
Many are the impossible things we've undertaken,
many the hard beds, whether great admiral
or common seaman. May you never find me a harsh judge
of what you've done, or hard to please,
or severe in any way whatever.
But you will find me kind   400
and very young,
now I am freed from all worries.
We have wasted time enough
in countermarching on parade,
heavy with shield and spear.
Now tell us what you would
particularly like us to do?
Kind Fate has made you
our lord today.

*(Trygaeus moves away from the chorus and examines the largest heap of
stones. While he is doing this, Hermes strolls on
stage and watches him with increasing horror.)*

TRYGAEUS

Now let's give some thought to this: how are we going to move
the stones?   410

HERMES

Unclean, useless man, what are you thinking of?

TRYGAEUS
    Nothing bad, everything according to Killikon.

HERMES
    O evil spirit, thou are lost!

TRYGAEUS
    Well, that's ok, if that's how my lot falls out.
    For, being Hermes, I know You will do it with dice.

HERMES
    You are lost. You shall perish utterly.

TRYGAEUS
    What day?

HERMES
    This very moment!

TRYGAEUS
    But I'm no way ready for it:
    No bread, no cheese—a condemned man needs his food.   420

HERMES
    You are rendered over to judgment!

TRYGAEUS
    Now, how did this blessing come on me,
    and me not know?

HERMES
    Dost thou not know that Zeus has proclaimed death
    for any found digging for Her?

TRYGAEUS
    Now has it come that I must die?

HERMES
> You can be sure of it.

TRYGAEUS
> You'll have to lend me some cash for a pig.
> I've got to be initiate before I die.

HERMES
> O Zeus of the thunder, Zeus of the lightning!   430

TRYGAEUS
> But I beg you, Master
> don't denounce me before the gods.

HERMES
> I shall not stay quiet.

TRYGAEUS
> Nay, by those burnt offerings that I brought You
> gladly and with a full heart when I came.

HERMES
> But look here: it's me will get done by Zeus
> if I don't shriek and make a row.

TRYGAEUS
> Wonderful Hermes, I beseech You, do not shriek.
> *(turning to Chorus)*
> Anyway what's the matter with you lot? Why are you
> standing there in a total panic, you fools,   440
> and not saying anything? If you say nothing He will yell.

CHORUS
> Do not, Lord Hermes, do not, do not, do not,
> do not do it, if You would know

the taste of pig,
and indeed of my sucking pig,
but consider this a trifle in the great fabric of the universe.

TRYGAEUS

Do You not hear their sweet blandishments, my Lord and
Master?

CHORUS

Be not hostile to our entreaties.
Do not hinder our removing Her from here.
But, most gracious lover of men,   450
most munificent of spirits,
if the haughty hair and brows of Peisander sicken you
we will worship You in every way,
with sacrifice and mighty procession,
and, Master, we will bless You forever.

TRYGAEUS

Come on, please, show them a bit of pity over Her.

HERMES

They appear to be more my thieves than they were before.

TRYGAEUS

And I tell you, there is something big, something really awful
going on: there's a plot against all the Gods.

HERMES

Ok, tell me. I trust you that far, I suppose.   460

TRYGAEUS

Look, we sacrifice to *You*, but the Barbarians
sacrifice to *Them*. So: *They* are putting all their thoughts
to our destruction. And then they get everything.

HERMES

>So they embezzled bits of the days that used to be
>in their daily chariot run.

TRYGAEUS

>By Zeus, beloved Hermes, help us over Her,
>help us to extract Her.
>And we will celebrate the great festivals of the gods,
>each and every rite of every god—
>the mysteries of Hermes, the adoration of Zeus, the Adonis.   470
>And the cities You have saved from ill
>will sacrifice one and all to their redeemer Hermes.

(gives Hermes a gold cup)

>I give You this gold thing that You may have due drink offering.

HERMES

>Well, I'm always inclined to mercy when there's gold.
>So, next, your little job, my friends.
>Make a start with your spades, and then
>lift out the boulders quick as you can.

CHORUS

>We undertake this work. Whatever, wisest of gods,
>it is necessary to do, tell us,
>craftsman and smith,   480
>and You shall not find us lacking in any way.

TRYGAEUS

>Come on, quick, hold out the libation cup
>so we may undertake this work secure in our relations with the
>>>>gods.

HERMES

>Pour away, pour away,
>and pray to me nicely, pray to me nicely.

TRYGAEUS
> And as we make our libations let us pray
> that all blessings shall come on Greece today,
> that our bonds shall be released willingly
> and no man bear a shield again.

CHORUS
> No, by Zeus, but pass his days in Peace   490
> poking the coal with his girl beside him.

TRYGAEUS
> Now he that thinks that war is better,
> may he never, Lord Dionysus, cease
> from taking arrow barbs out of his elbows.

CHORUS
> And if there is someone who fancies himself
> in command of cavalry for the booty,
> may his battles go badly, Lady Athena,
> worse than Cleonymus.

TRYGAEUS
> And if there is a spear salesman,
> a trader in shields who for the sake of lucre   500
> wants another war, let him fall into the hands of brigands
> and eat just barley.

CHORUS
> And if some general does not intend to assist us,
> but to desert like a common slave,
> let him be beaten before his pain on the wheel.
> Great blessings are come upon us. Hi! Hi!
> Let us sing a song of joy.

TRYGAEUS
>Leave out the beatings, and just say "Ho!"

CHORUS
>Hi! Hi! for this day "Hi" is the only thing I'll say.

TRYGAEUS
>O Hermes, O you Graces and you Hours, Aphrodite, Desire . . .   510

CHORUS
>Not Ares?

TRYGAEUS
>No.

CHORUS
>Or his sister in war?

TRYGAEUS
>No.
>*(During this exchange the members of the Chorus have attached ropes to*
>>*the stones, and now they have lined up ready to*
>>*extract them.)*

CHORUS
>Now, everyone, pull, heave hard on the ropes!
>*(It is noticeable, however, that those in the cleaner town clothes are*
>>*standing at the back and not making much effort.*
>>*It is the farmers in their dirty tunics who stand at*
>>*the front and work.)*

HERMES
>Oh, heave!

CHORUS
>Heave more!

HERMES
Oh, heave!

CHORUS
More, more heaving!

HERMES
Oh heave, oh heave!   520

TRYGAEUS
But not all the chaps are making the same effort.
They aren't all pulling together. Some are just yelling.
Our Theban friends will really have cause to moan.
(He wanders over toward one group, waving a branch he has picked up.)

HERMES
Now heave!

TRYGAEUS
Oh, heave!

CHORUS
But you lot ought to pull too.

TRYGAEUS
Why don't I pull: I think it through.
I attack any problem with zeal.

CHORUS
So why are we still stuck?

TRYGAEUS
Lamax, you sit there and do us wrong.   530
Man, we do not require your evil spirit.

HERMES

> And the Argives you know don't pull like they used to:
> they have grown hard of heart and laugh;
> they get paid by each side for their grain.

TRYGAEUS

> But the Laconians pull well and like men.

HERMES

> But it's noticeable it's only those who wear the wood shackles
> of prisoners who give their all.
> The ones still in armor do not pull.

TRYGAEUS

> The men of Megara do not try at all.
> They were mean and like stray dogs pulling flesh off a bone,   540
> and now Zeus has brought them down and they hunger.

CHORUS

> We aren't doing much, but with a single spirit
> all as one we must make the effort now.

HERMES

> Oh, pull!

TRYGAEUS

> Pull more!

HERMES

> Oh, pull!

TRYGAEUS

> Pull, by Zeus!

CHORUS

> We're shifting it a bit.

TRYGAEUS

    Dreadful: some aren't pulling,
    holding back. I'll tickle your ribs,   550
    you Argives!

HERMES

    Pull now!

TRYGAEUS

    Oh, pull!

CHORUS

    Some of you are still against us.

TRYGAEUS

    You that crave the strange food of peace,
    heave with all your strength!

CHORUS

    But they are hindering us again.

HERMES

    Men of Megara, what—no heaving! To the crows, then!
    The Goddess remembers you and hates.
    You were first to anoint Her statue with garlic.   560
    Athenians, I tell you, you must stop,
    for you are doing it according to the rules.
    If you really want to haul Her out,
    step back a little in the direction of the ocean.

TRYGAEUS

    Come on, you lot. The farmers alone can pull her out.
(Everyone except the farmers steps away.)

HERMES

    The whole thing is going much better with you doing it.

CHORUS

He says it's beginning to happen. With your whole heart now!

TRYGAEUS

The farmers are pulling her out, and no one else.

CHORUS OF FARMERS

Now heave, all together, heave.

And no one not of one mind.   570

Now we are getting there.

Now we must not slacken,

but heave on like true men.

This is it, this is Her.

Oh heh ho heave, all together heave,

heh ho heave, heh ho heave,

Oh heave, heh ho heave, heh ho heave,

all together heave!

(The rocks are pulled back to reveal the large statue that is the Goddess of
Peace and two beautiful young women: Opora, the
incarnation of Harvest and Autumn, and Madame
Ambassador, who would be dressed respectably if it
were not for her very low neckline.)

TRYGAEUS

O Mistress, producer of grapes, how am I to speak to You?

I wish I could clutch many-shaped vowels out of air   580

with which to address You, but I have none.

Dear Opora, and you, Madame Ambassador.

What a face you have, Madame Ambassador.

What breath, so sweet from your inner depth,

sweetest one, so different from the odors of conscription.

HERMES

Bit different from a soldier's kitbag, certainly.

TRYGAEUS

    I hate the basket smell of men in the power of Hate.
    It is sharp with eructation of onions.
    But this is not that, but Her of harvest,
    entertainment, the feasts of Dionysus,   590
    the playing of flutes and tragedies,
    the lilt of Sophocles, the little words
    of Euripides.

HERMES

    How could you slander Her so?
    She is a true poet and loathes
    the little words of rhetoric.

TRYGAEUS

    This is She of ivy, of wine strained through the cloth,
    of lambs bleating, and full breasted women
    hurrying into the fields;
    of the slave girl drunk, and the bottle drained,   600
    and everything else that is wonderful.

HERMES

    And now come and look: the cities chatter one to another,
    for they have made truce, and are happy, and laugh.
    And yet the gods have made their eyes swell,
    and they hold their cupping glasses tight.

TRYGAEUS

    And look at our audience—
    you can tell each man's trade by his look.

HERMES

    Such things!
    Don't you see the maker of battle helmet crests
    tearing his hair? And the maker of hoes   610
    has just let one go at the sharpener of swords.

TRYGAEUS

And don't you see how glad is the sickle maker
as he teases the maker of spears?

HERMES

And now make proclamation that the farmers can depart.

TRYGAEUS

Harken, O people: all farmers to go,
to take up their implements, to enter the fields
with all possible speed, without spear, sword, or violence.
Because the whole world is full of the joys of peace,
as you go to the fields to work, sing songs of praise.

CHORUS OF FARMERS

O day delightful to those good in heart and to the agricultural!   620
Because I am glad I am willing to speak of vines.
And there are those fig trees I planted when I was younger.
There is joy in my heart that I am to see them after so long.

TRYGAEUS

But first we must pray to this god of female form,
who has freed us from the crests and gorgon shields of war.
And then, before we slip off into the country,
we must buy (it always comes in handy) some salt fish or meat.

HERMES

O Poseidon, how lovely their procession—
tight and stern as festival cakes!

TRYGAEUS

By Zeus, their hoes are bright as their armor used to be,   630
and their forks outgleam the sun.
Just right for those who are to clear between vines.
Indeed, I am eager myself to get into the fields
and break up soil that has been so long unhoed.

But we must remember, comrades,
our ways of old
that She brought to us:
those olden things,
figs and myrtles,
new wine in its sweetness,   640
and violets by the well,
and olives which we have
so long desired.
For all these, now,
let us address the Goddess.

CHORUS

Greeting, greeting, dearest,
that are come among us to our joy.
We are full of desire for You,
wanting some godliness
to lead us back into our fields.   650
O desirable You brought us great things,
and we ground out the life of farmers
in every aspect.
Only Thou assisted us.
Many things we enjoyed
in the former time
through your kind, free bounty.
There was wheat and salvation for all farmers.
And for you, Goddess,
the vine plant and young fig   660
and whatever grows
shall laugh
and be glad at your coming.

But where was she in her long absence from us.
Tell us, you best informed of Gods.
*(Hermes takes up a central position, and addresses the gathering. The
jokiness has gone; there is a new seriousness.)*

HERMES

>Ah, you shrewd countrymen, you'll have to go
>through quite a digression, if you want to know
>about the expulsion of Peace.
>It was Phidias who first did Her wrong.
>Then Pericles panicked in case he should get a share   670
>of the bad luck you dish out
>when your temper's amuck. Before he suffered
>anything, he inflamed the city
>and scattered the little spark of his Megara vote.
>And he roused such a war with the smoke of that fire
>that every Greek—come here, come there—had occasion to
>>   weep.
>And when this was heard the vine boiled over
>and cask gushed on cask
>according to the lashes of the rite.
>But there was none to bring ecstasy to end,   680
>none to manifest light.

TRYGAEUS

>By Apollo, I never knew anything about this.
>I did not know Phidias was involved with her.

CHORUS

>Me neither, till now. So that's why she's so lovely—
>because she was involved with the sculptor. All that's stayed
>>   hidden.

HERMES

>And then they understood—the cities of your dominion—
>that you were disputing mastery with yourselves,
>and in malice. And then they began to struggle with you
>over anything, fearing your tribute;
>and won over Sparta with great bribes.   690
>And those greedy mistreaters of guests,
>to their shame, put Her out, and embraced War.
>But this greed brought ill to countrymen,

for the galley of vengeance
consumed the figs of righteous men.

TRYGAEUS

All too true, for they cut down my gray fig tree
that I sowed and I reared.

CHORUS

By Zeus, oh, by Zeus, true indeed! They chucked a stone
on my biggest grain bin and smashed it.

HERMES

And then clansfolk flocked from the fields.   700
The way they were sold beyond their comprehension,
but without grape stones, and longing for figs,
they looked to the speakers of the assembly, who
understood you were poor, famished, and lacked
household goods, and thrust out the Goddess with pitchforks
and imprecations, though the light of her desire
for her land was bright and constant.
And there was trouble for any ally
who was rich and important,
and any that mentioned Spartan generals were guilty.   710
And you leapt like a hound at the kill.
The city is pale with the judgment of fear.
Slanderers against her consumed ravenously.
And then foreigners, recognizing the roots
of their misfortune, filled the mouths
of the originators of these obloquies with gold,
so they became rich while Hellas reaped
what you chose to forget.
And he that wrought this was a tanner.

TRYGAEUS

Stop it, stop it, Lord Hermes, don't say it,   720
but let him, whoever he is,
reside down *there*.

For he doesn't belong with us: he's yours.
Whatever You call him—
jack of all trades,
spreader of rumors, slanderer,
agitator, stirrer.
You'll call him the lot,
now he's yours.
But why are You silent, my Queen, speak to me.   730

HERMES
But She won't talk in front of all these spectators.
For She is full of anger toward this city.

TRYGAEUS
But won't She whisper to You by yourself?

HERMES *(to the statue)*
Speak your inmost thoughts to me.
Come, who of all females hates shield straps most.
(pauses as if listening)
Yes, I understand.
(to Trygaeus and the Chorus)
                            What's Athens done? I'll explain.
You listen. This is Her cause to moan.
She observes that after the Pylos campaign
She came by Her choice with a chest
of treaties for this city,   740
and three times the Assembly turned them down.

TRYGAEUS
We were wrong. But let us have your pardon.
Our common sense got tangled up in shield hide.

HERMES
Now listen: this is what She wants to know.
Who here had most evil in his mind against Her,
and who loves Her and desires no war?

TRYGAEUS
    Cleonymus showed a fine blessed spirit.

HERMES
    And what does Cleonymus have to say
    on the subject of war?

TRYGAEUS
    An excellent spirit, except he is not,   750
    as they always say, his father's son.
    For when he went soldiering
    he proved a born thrower away of equipment.

HERMES
    Now listen again. This is what She has to say.
    Who holds sway at the assembly stone?

TRYGAEUS
    Hyperbolos has the ear of the people.
    But what is She doing? Why does She not look at us?

HERMES
    She turns from her people because she is troubled
    that such a dreadful leader was elected.

TRYGAEUS
    There wasn't a lot of point, but the people,   760
    in real trouble and leaderless,
    chose this man in the hope of salvation.

HERMES
    How does this help the beloved city?

TRYGAEUS
    It leads to more informed discussion.

HERMES
    How!

TRYGAEUS

    Well it so happens he was a lamp maker,
    so, where we used to do our business in the dark
    now we discuss it in the light.

HERMES

    Yea! Yea!
    What She has instructed me to ask . . .   770

TRYGAEUS

    What, what?

HERMES

    About all those things that were before Her going forth.
    First, how is Sophocles?

TRYGAEUS

    Oh quite happy. But he's undergone a wondrous change.

HERMES

    What, what?

TRYGAEUS

    Out of Sophocles, Simonides is born.

HERMES

    Simonides? How?

TRYGAEUS

    He's grown old and stale,
    and sails in a basket for greed.

HERMES

    Now what's that one up to? Cratinus, the wise?   780

TRYGAEUS

    Dead during a Spartan raid!

HERMES
> What was his end?

TRYGAEUS
> Ah, swooned away, for he could not stand
> the sight of a cask broken and the wine lost.
> But so much has happened in this city.
> Lady, we must never let You go again.

HERMES
> Come now, before these people take Opora
> for your wife, and in the fields of the common lands
> raise up a vine of your stock.

TRYGAEUS
> Dearest, come here and give us a kiss.   790
> *(He hesitates, though Opora approaches eagerly.)*
> But Lord Hermes, have I got it right?
> Surely there will be harm for generations
> if I lie down with Opora?

HERMES
> Not if you make yourself the right potion.
> But, quick as possible, take Madame Ambassador
> along to the Council, and her rightful place.

TRYGAEUS
> Oh, how blessed is the Council
> to have Madame Ambassador as a member!
> How much sauce you will scoff in the space of three days.
> What quantities of tripe, what masses of meat.   800
> But, my dear Hermes, it's fondest goodbyes.

HERMES
> And, my dear mortal, it's fond farewell
> and remember me always.

TRYGAEUS
> Beetle, beetle! Home, home! Time to go!

HERMES
> He's not here any longer.

TRYGAEUS
> Where has he gone off to?

HERMES
> He is departed with the chariot of Zeus,
> he bears the thunder.

TRYGAEUS
> How does the poor creature get fed?

HERMES
> His grub is the ambrosia of Ganymede.   810

TRYGAEUS
> So how am I to get down?

HERMES
> Happily and well: for you shall go
> at the side of the Goddess.

TRYGAEUS
> Now come on now, you girls,
> quick! get in with me:
> young men lust for you
> and would make children.

(Trygaeus and the two girls exit via a trap door with the Statue of Peace,
waved off by the chorus, who perform while the
stage is cleared behind them.)

CHORUS
>Have a good journey! But in the interval we hand over the stage
>in safe keeping to the attendants according to custom,
>for thieves lurk about stages in numbers, heads down,   820
>doing bad things, so play your part manfully,
>while we exposit to the spectators
>the right road of words and the soul.

>It's for the umpire to strike hard if any poet of the comedy
>should praise himself to the audience in the anapestic address.
>But if ever, Daughter of Zeus, it is reasonable, it is
>this best of chorus trainers and finest born of men
>who should be called wise and our teacher.
>For he alone put a stop to the ceaseless battles of wit,
>and puns on minute matters, and interesting struggles with lice.   830
>And the Heracles all kneading bread, and their terrible hungers;
>and the swindles, and the flights, and the pursuits, and the
>   beatings.
>And after being driven forth in dishonor, he gave the slaves their
>   freedom,
>and always they entered in tears, and it went something like this.
>A fellow slave would jeer at their stripes and say:
>"Poor unfortunate, what happened to your skin?
>Did the whip get you on the ribs, then,
>like a great army felling the trees of the plain?"
>He removed this load of stupidity, these jokes of lesser men.
>He made for us a great art, a city, and a citadel   840
>of great thoughts and purposes, and jokes not guffawed in the
>   fields.
>None of the idiotic portrayals of the semblance of men and
>   women,
>but with the passion of Heracles assailed great matters,
>passed through the fearsome smells of the tannery,
>and crossed through the minds of mud.

CHORUS LEADER/ARISTOPHANES
    And my first fight was with the sharpest toothed monster of all.
    And the light of his eyes was dreadful as the prostitution of
           Cynna.
    And a hundred flatterers moaned in a circle of snakes round his
           head.
    And he had the voice of a mountain stream, begetting
           destruction.
    And the scent of a seal, and the unwashed balls of a goblin,   850
    and the rear end of an oven. I was not afraid at this wondrous
           sight,
    but fought for You, and fought for the Islands. I was your
           bastion.
    I did this first. I did not cruise the gymnasium
    on the lookout for boys, but picked up my clobber and went,
    having done little harm, and given much fun, and done what was
           needed.

    And you men, and you boys,
    must be of my party,
    and baldheaded men
    must especially exert themselves
    for my victory.   860
    And all shall speak
    of my victory
    at the concluding party:
    "Take baldy, give baldy
    his nuts, and take them not away
    from the man that has the brow
    of the poets of nobility."

CHORUS
    Muse that expelled war, dance with me that love You.
    Sing us the weddings of gods. Cry us the feasts of mortals
    and the joys of half-gods as You were meant to do from Time's
           beginning.   870

CHORUS LEADER

But if Crabby comes and asks if his boys can dance,
harken not nor succor them,
but regard them as housebred quails,
dancers with necks like a soldier's knapsack,
cousins of dwarves, hammer chippings,
stage machinery makers.
And if the father says,
"the play went as well as could be expected,"
let the polecat strangle him at midnight.

CHORUS

And these are the songs of the Muses of bright hair   880
that the wisehearted poet should sing,
just as the swallow sits and shrieks
his Spring noise. And no chorus
for Morsimos, no chorus for Melanthios,
the gratings of whose words I have heard.
He, he and his brother had the chorus of the tragedy:
gorgons of vegetarian tendency,
desirers of skates and harpies,
pursuers of ancient women.
Unclean!   890
Armpits with the foetor of goats,
bringers of fish to a dark end.
Let them be spat upon from head to toe,
and then my Muse, my Goddess,
let You and me enjoy the holiday.

> (*Exit chorus. The stage is briefly dark, and a strange shadowy music
> plays. The lights gradually go up to reveal Trygaeus, once again
> in the courtyard of his house, along with Opora and Madame
> Ambassador. The scene is as at the beginning, except that there is
> no beetle.*)

TRYGAEUS

Such an effort to get up to the gods.
I certainly put my legs through it.

And everything down here so slight,
viewed from up there. And from Heaven you seemed wholly
        wicked,
but down here you're a whole lot worse.   900

FIRST SERVANT *(running in from the house)*
    Master, is it you, are you back?

TRYGAEUS
    I am, as I was prophesied.

FIRST SERVANT
    What happened?

TRYGAEUS
    Long was the road my legs must undergo!

FIRST SERVANT
    Come now, tell me all about it.

TRYGAEUS
    What?

FIRST SERVANT
    You see any men swanning about in the sky
    except yourself?

TRYGAEUS
    No—just a few spirits
    of dithyrambic poets.   910

FIRST SERVANT
    And what were they up to?

TRYGAEUS
    Going about in ones and twos looking for odes,
    airy beings floating on the breezes of midday.

FIRST SERVANT
> And is it like they say up there up in the sky—
> that a star is born when someone dies?

TRYGAEUS
> Certainly.

FIRST SERVANT
> And who's the star right now?

TRYGAEUS
> Ion, the Chian, who composed
> a song to the Dawn down here,
> so when he got up there the other stars   920
> called him "the Star of Morning."

FIRST SERVANT
> And what are those stars that fall
> and burn in their swiftness?

TRYGAEUS
> Oh, those are the better-off stars
> on their way back from a meal.
> They have lanterns, and fire in the lanterns.
> *(He takes Opora, who is hovering uncertainly in the corner, by the*
> *hand.)*
> But grab this one, and take her inside, quick!
> And fill the tub to overflowing,
> and make sure the water's hot!
> And make a bed for me and her,   930
> a rightful marriage bed.
> And when you've done all that,
> come back here.
> *(Madame Ambassador takes Trygaeus by the hand rather demurely.)*
> In the meanwhile,
> I will hand over this one to the Council.

FIRST SERVANT

> Where did you get these girls?

TRYGAEUS

> Where? Oh from Heaven.

FIRST SERVANT

> I wouldn't give much for the gods—
> if they'd got brothels
> like us men down here.   940

TRYGAEUS

> No, but there are some gods get their living from them.

FIRST SERVANT

> Come along, woman. Tell me, have I got to feed her?

TRYGAEUS

> No way! She won't want bread—
> wheat or barley.
> She's used to licking ambrosia among gods.

FIRST SERVANT

> Best make something for her to lick down here then.
> *(Exit Opora with the servant. The farmers of the Chorus in the heavenly
>   scene reenter together with their wives, but without
>   the workmen of the town.)*

CHORUS

> Fortunate, ancient man,
> that have achieved
> all that you foresaw.

TRYGAEUS

> What, then, when you see me   950
> in the bright raiment of a bridegroom?

CHORUS

    You shall be worthy of emulation: old,
    but anointed with myrrh
    as when you were young.

TRYGAEUS

    All right, but what when I possess the tits
    that belong to everyone?

CHORUS

    That would appear to be more fortunate
    than the contortions
    of the chorus of Mr. Crab.

TRYGAEUS

    How does one justify such praise? I suppose   960
    I passed through the foundations of Earth
    with a beetle and saved Greece.
    And everyone is back in the fields,
    safe to work, and safe to laze.
(Enter the first servant in a hurry.)

FIRST SERVANT

    She's had her bath, and her bum's gorgeous!
    The cake's nearly baked, and the puddings almost ready.
    All's done. All we need's a prick.

TRYGAEUS

    I'd better hurry up, then, and hand over Madame Ambassador,
    and get everything done with the Council.

FIRST SERVANT

    What's that? What do you say?   970
    Is she that Madame Ambassador
    we heard on the feast of Brauron
    and made our submission to?

TRYGAEUS
Quite right: the one you can't get to stop.

FIRST SERVANT
She has permission for five years' fucking.

TRYGAEUS *(to the audience)*
Now is there anyone out there I can trust—
someone to look after her and take her to the Council?
(to the servant)
Heh, what are you writing?

FIRST SERVANT
Shouldn't say, but at the Isthmian feast
I am going to lay siege to her tent with my prick.   980

TRYGAEUS
What, no one's willing to look after her? Come on, then!
I'll have to go down myself and take you to them.

FIRST SERVANT
Someone's beckoning.

TRYGAEUS
Who?

FIRST SERVANT
Who? Ariphrades wants her brought along by him.

TRYGAEUS
But after he's had a go
her sauce will be all drunk up.
*(He leads Madame Ambassador opposite the seats reserved for the
                    Parliamentarians.)*
Council, Committee, behold, Madame Ambassador!
(She throws one leg up in the air, and lifts her robes to reveal nakedness.)

Consider what blessings this coming will bring.
Now that her leg has been raised up in the air for you,   990
proclaim a festival.
(gestures to her genitals)
Behold the quality
of her cooking shack, in which things go on the stove
at once, and where before the War
the Council had a place to put its saucepans.
And then there shall be games
and a wholly beautiful tomorrow:
and wrestling—feet on the ground
or on all fours—and plenty of crooked throws,
hands on the knees. And wrestle-boxing   1000
after vigorous anointing,
and fist happening to hit foul and in the groin.
Then on the third day let us have the equestrian events—
horse on horse over-reaching,
chariots getting caught on each other and overturned,
puffed and out of breath the winners,
and the boyfriends taking a nap
and troubled by indigestion,
and so many charioteers fallen, fallen in the plains!
But he whose right it is to introduce Madame Ambassador   1010
to this committee, how happy is his lot.
*(There is a distinctly awkward pause. A Parliamentarian comes forward
              and whispers in Trygaeus' ear. He produces a purse
              rather discreetly, and hands it over.)*
But not if someone did not give you a little something
in consideration for your undertaking the transaction!
Otherwise, I'd have found you saying "nothing doing today."
*(Madame Ambassador suddenly abandons her posture in view of her
              new public role, and ventures into the audience,
              intent on the public good.)*

CHORUS
How good and how simple is this man
in the eyes of every citizen.

TRYGAEUS

When you have got the harvest in, you will understand
much better what manner of man I am.

CHORUS

Already for sure you are proclaimed
savior to all mankind.   1020

TRYGAEUS

You'll say it for true
when you drink a cup of young wine.

CHORUS

The Gods apart, you shall be called first among beings.

TRYGAEUS

I am of great value to you,
Trygaeus born in Athmone,
that set free the city from terrible things—
and the rustic clans—
and put a stop to Hyperbolos.

FIRST SERVANT

So what's next?

TRYGAEUS

What other than to set up a statue of pots to her?   1030

FIRST SERVANT

What? Pots for Peace—like we offer that crook Hermes?

TRYGAEUS

So what do you think? Would a nice fat ox do?

FIRST SERVANT

An ox? No way, don't need that sort of help.

TRYGAEUS
Or a pig, huge and fat?

FIRST SERVANT
No way, no way.

TRYGAEUS
Why?

FIRST SERVANT
In case we get piggish-souled—like that fellow Hogg.

TRYGAEUS
So what do you think we should use out of what's left?

FIRST SERVANT
Baa!

TRYGAEUS
Baa?   1040

FIRST SERVANT
Yes, by Zeus.

TRYGAEUS
But that's Ionic.

FIRST SERVANT
Extremely useful, that. For if
some chap in the Assembly
starts on about War,
everyone there
in their alarm and worry
shall say "Baa!"
in the best Ionic fashion.

TRYGAEUS

    Very good!   1050

FIRST SERVANT

    And so shall their mildness be.

    And our behavior to each other shall be like lambs

    and to our allies we'll be even nicer.

TRYGAEUS

    Quick! Get us a sheep!

    I will get an altar ready for the sacrifice.

(Exit first servant.)

CHORUS

    So, when a god wills and Fate accomplishes,

    there is a way that is right, thing fits to thing,

    and all is in due order.

TRYGAEUS

    All is now manifest, and the altar before the gates.

CHORUS

    Proceed now in this matter,   1060

    while the gods utter a breeze

    to restrain blood-feud and war,

    and beyond a doubt some spirit

    directs us into grace.

TRYGAEUS

    The basket is here, and the barley of sacrifice,

    and the wreath, and the knife,

    and we have a fire.

    We lack nothing except a sheep.

CHORUS LEADER

    Why so little effort?

    If Chairis sees this   1070

he'll play his flute before you ask,
and he'll get so puffed and blown
you'll have to pay.
*(During this chorus a sheep is brought onto the stage, and brought with
some difficulty to Trygaeus by the first servant.)*

TRYGAEUS

    Come on! Take basket and jar,
    circle the altar with speed left to right.

FIRST SERVANT

    Now look here, you'll have to tell me something else to do:
    I've already been and gone round.

TRYGAEUS

    Then bring me the torch from the altar,
    and I will dip it in the water.
(to the sheep)
    Quick! shake yourself while you can.   1080
(to the servant)
    Bring out the holy barley, but first give it to me
    and cleanse yourself.
*(First servant cleanses himself by throwing several buckets of water in
various directions.)*
    And when all that is done,
    hurl these sacred grains among the spectators.

FIRST SERVANT *(who has been standing in some bemusement, not actually
doing anything, and trying to interrupt)*
    But look! It's done.

TRYGAEUS
    What! The Distribution's done already?

FIRST SERVANT
    Yes by Hermes, for there is none among them
    lacks seed in his groin.

TRYGAEUS
     But the women haven't any!

FIRST SERVANT
     But they're in hope   1090
     the men will give them some of theirs.

TRYGAEUS *(making the best of a bad job)*
     Now let us pray. Who is present?
     Are there good men, and many?

FIRST SERVANT
     Bring hither and offer. There are many and good.

TRYGAEUS
     Do you acknowledge these men to be good?

FIRST SERVANT
     Yea, for though they have had much water poured on them
     they stand on their ground and make their dance.

TRYGAEUS
     But let us pray with all speed, let us pray.

     Queen of Goddesses, worthy of worship,
     Mistress of dance, Lady of weddings,   1100
     receive our offering.

FIRST SERVANT
     Receive it, so worthy of respect,
     act not like women that commit adultery,
     and turn aside and make themselves small
     before the doors of their lovers,
     and if any look on them with suspicion,
     turn aside. Don't ever do things like that to us.

TRYGAEUS

    Indeed, by Zeus, but deny not the holy grain
    of your nobility to us who love you
    and have languished ten years and three.   1110
    Release us from the ill winds of War,
    and we will name you "Battle-Releaser."
    End our suspicion in its elegance,
    our babblings against friends.
    Make us peoples of Greece
    one, as in the foretime.
    Make fast our friendship.
    Temper our souls
    with mildness and forgiveness.
    And may our market be full   1120
    of great fruit, and good.
    Cucumbers sprung early, apples, pomegranates,
    and nice little cloaks to cover the slaves.
    And brought down from Thebes for our delight
    the goose, the duck, the pigeon, and the sandpiper.
    And baskets come from Copais.
    And everyone milling round in a crowd,
    in a tizz to buy:
    Morykos, Teleas, Glaucetes
    and each and every gourmand.   1130
    And let Melanthios come late
    into the market, and what he wants be sold,
    and he wail—a true monody of Medea:
    "Lost, all lost, bereaved:
    my beloved is brought to bed among beet."
    And so men shall have cause to rejoice.
    Grant us all this for which we pray.

FIRST SERVANT

    Take up the sword of sacrifice. Be as a cook
    and slaughter the sheep.

TRYGAEUS
But that's not the custom.   1140

FIRST SERVANT
How come?

TRYGAEUS *(fiddling with some bits of firewood)*
Dead offerings are not pleasing to Peace,
nor blood on her altar. But take the sheep in
and make sacrifice, and cut meat from the thighs
and bring them out. That way the sheep
stays reserved for our patron.
(Exit first servant carrying the sheep into the house.)

CHORUS
You, by the doors, bring the wood
and place it quickly;
there is general advantage in this.
*(Several people rush onto the stage, bearing firewood, which they kindle
and set fire to. Trygaeus looks increasingly
indignant.)*

TRYGAEUS
Don't you feel I'm placing the firewood   1150
as a true prophet would?

CHORUS
Not at all. We look to you
who have all that appertains to wisdom.
Do you not feel that all the cooked meat
belongs to him who is approved in wisdom
and has a soul of daring and invention?

TRYGAEUS
Well, the kindling is certainly blazing,
and the Fortune Teller chokes.

I will make ready a table,
and a boy shall not be lacking.   1160

CHORUS
    Is there any will not admire
    this man, who with much travail
    preserved the holy city?
    His renown as our savior
    shall not cease.

FIRST SERVANT *(entering covered with blood, fat and smoke)*
    All done. Shove on this bit of thigh I've brought.
    Me, I'll go and get the guts, and the incense and so on.

TRYGAEUS
    And I'll put my mind to this. But why so long?

FIRST SERVANT
    Well, look, I'm here. No way have I kept you back.

TRYGAEUS
    Take charge of the roasting. Heh look, there's someone coming. 1170
    He's got laurel all round his head.
    Now who is he?

FIRST SERVANT
    Seems like a beggar.
    Oh no, it's a prophet.

TRYGAEUS
    No, by Zeus, its Hierocles that's coming—
    that monger of oracles from Oreus.
    (Hierocles enters dressed most bizarrely in the skins of sacrificial victims.)

FIRST SERVANT
    Now what will he prophesy?

TRYGAEUS
Its plain he's against the truce.

FIRST SERVANT
No! He's just smelt the sacrifice.

TRYGAEUS
Let's seem not to see him.   1180

FIRST SERVANT
Quite right!
*(They huddle over the sacrifice, looking away from Hierocles, who walks
          around them trying to see their faces. He gives up,
          and makes the proper inquiry.)*

HIEROCLES
Who makes this present sacrifice, and to what gods?

TRYGAEUS *(to first servant, who is pulling off bits of meat and eating them)*
Keep quiet, and lay off the loin.

HIEROCLES
Will you not explain the object of your sacrifice?
That tail's nicely done.

FIRST SERVANT *(in ecstasy over the meat)*
Nice, and more than nice, my lady, my Queen of Peace.

HIEROCLES *(making the correct invocation)*
Now let us begin: offer the pure thing.

TRYGAEUS *(good manners getting slightly the better of him)*
Better when it's cooked.

HIEROCLES
But it's already cooked.

TRYGAEUS
>You're in too much of a hurry, whoever you are.   1190
>Now it's time to carve. Now where did the table get put?
>Bring the drink-offering in fulfillment of the truce.

HIEROCLES
>The tongue is first to be cut.

TRYGAEUS
>I know. But do you understand
>what we have achieved?

HIEROCLES
>I will when you tell me.

TRYGAEUS
>Don't interrupt. Our sacrifice is to Peace.

HIEROCLES
>You unhappy men—foolish mortal!

TRYGAEUS
>If you say so!

HIEROCLES
>You are feckless. You disobey the inclination of the gods.   1200
>You that have made these treaties have the blue eyes of apes!

FIRST SERVANT
>Bull! All bull!

TRYGAEUS
>How come you're laughing?

FIRST SERVANT
>Well, I liked his blue-eyed apes.

HIEROCLES

Shy birds of the sea, that put your trust
in the wily soul and crafty mind of the fox.

TRYGAEUS

May your lungs be as hot as this meat that cooks.

HIEROCLES

If the Nymphs in their holiness have not been having Bakis on,
and Bakis has not been imposing on common men, or (to say it
again)
the Nymphs have not been having Bakis on—   1210

TRYGAEUS

Ruination to you if you don't stop it about Bakis!

HIEROCLES

Otherwise, no final decree that the bonds of Peace are loosed.
You've got to have this first.

TRYGAEUS *(standing over the cauldron)*

Now I sprinkle with salt this offering.

HIEROCLES

It is not the kind intention of the Gods in their blessedness
that the noise of battle should cease,
not till wolf and lamb are as one.

TRYGAEUS

What, you silly chump, wolf and lamb to be one?

HIEROCLES

As the beetle farts to cover its retreat,
and the linnet bears blind children in the haste of its flight,   1220
so is there need for Peace to be made.

TRYGAEUS

Now how does that affect us? Is war never to end?
Are we to be worn down in the struggle for supremacy
when we might have a confederation in Hellas?

HIEROCLES

You will never make the crab walk straight.

TRYGAEUS

You shall dine no more in the places of committee.
You shall achieve no more with your roguery.

HIEROCLES

You cannot soften the spines of the sea urchin.

TRYGAEUS

Will you never stop imposing on the Athenians!

HIEROCLES

What oracle taught you to spoil the thighs meant for the gods?   1230

TRYGAEUS

This is the best oracle of them all, made by Homer himself:

"When the fearful cloud of war was driven away,
they brought back Peace and made her a sacrifice,
and burned the thighs, and consumed the lights,
and made libations; and I was the leader on that road.
and the shining cup was not offered to the man of false words."

HIEROCLES

I have no part in these: they are not true prophecies spoke by the
                    Sybil.

TRYGAEUS

But this I tell you, by Zeus, was what wise Homer worthily
                    uttered:

"Beyond tie of kin or force of custom is the landless man
that loves the horror of civil war."   1240

HIEROCLES

Beware, indeed, lest your soul undergo
the long intended trickeries of the kite.

TRYGAEUS *(to the servant)*

Better take note of this,
this oracle is ominous for the lights!
Pour the libation, and let's have some of those lights.

HIEROCLES

Well, if that's what you're thinking of,
I'll get stuck in myself.

TRYGAEUS

Pour the libation, pour it!

HIEROCLES

Pour some for me and hand us a bit of the guts.

TRYGAEUS

But that is no way the will of the blessed gods.   1250
This is the priority: I get a drink, you go away.
O Lady of Peace, let your strength be with us.

HIEROCLES

Bring the tongue over here.

TRYGAEUS

You take yours off somewhere else.

HIEROCLES

Pour!

TRYGAEUS *(throwing some rubbish from round the altar)*
Quick, grab this to go with your drink.

HIEROCLES
Will nobody give me any lights!

TRYGAEUS
No, I shall offer you none
till wolf and sheep be married.

HIEROCLES *(embracing Trygaeus by the knees)*
Please! By your knees!   1260

TRYGAEUS
No use, all this supplication.
For you shall not make soft the spines of the sea urchin.
Come on now, audience, come and have some lights with us.

HIEROCLES
What about me?

TRYGAEUS
Go eat your Sybil.

HIEROCLES
By the spirit of Earth you shall not partake of this alone.
But I'll grab a bit off you two. This is for everyone!

TRYGAEUS *(in a religious way to the servant, who is giving some thought to
                  pursuing Hierocles with a stick)*
Thump Bakis, thump Bakis.

HIEROCLES *(suddenly throwing up his hands as if to summon the Gods)*
Yea, I bear true witness!

TRYGAEUS *(to the servant)*
>   Me too! A glutton and a packet of tricks, that's you!   1270
>   Go on, bash him! *Thump him!* the rogue!

FIRST SERVANT *(handing the stick to Trygaeus with some ceremony to hit*
>   *Hierocles, who is now writhing on the floor in some*
>   *pain)*
>   No, you have a go. I'll get the skins off him
>   he got with his grabbing. Now, sacrificer,
>   won't you part with your skin.
> *(Layer after layer comes reluctantly off while Trygaeus continues to hit*
>   *Hierocles at every opportunity.)*
>   Didn't you hear? O Crow out of Oreus,
>   why don't you make a quick flight to Elysium?
> *(Exit Hierocles, pursued. The Chorus comes forward to fill the gap.)*

CHORUS
>   I am glad. I am happy
>   to be free of my helmet
>   and onions with cheese.
>   I have no love for battle,   1280
>   but prefer to be
>   by the fireside
>   with a few good friends,
>   with the logs burning bright
>   at the fag end of summer,
>   a hot charcoal dish
>   to spread the terebinth scent,
>   and acorns roasting,
>   and a little pleasure with Thratta
>   while my wife's at the bath.   1290

>   It's so pleasant when all's well, and the seed is growing nicely,
>   the god has sent us rain, and the neighbor's come to chat.
>   "Tell me, my friend, what does the situation demand?"
>   "I think I want to drink, now the god is pouring nicely."

So come on, you maids, and get roasting the beans
(we've got three quarts), and chuck in some barley,
and bring out the figs, and Syra call to Manes
to leave his allotment and come. For today is no time
for stripping off vine leaves or grubbing at roots:
the land is too wet. But bring me a thrush   1300
and bring me a siskin, and the first milk after the birth of the
        calf,
and four plates of hare, if the cat did not grab them last night.
For something stirred in the house last night
and I do not know what made that noise.
Three plates for us, my little child, and one for grandpa.
And beg myrtle boughs from Aeschinades,
and yell Charinades to join us if he's there.
And so we'll drink together
and increase our harvest prospects
in the presence of the God.   1310

And when the grasshopper
makes its pleasant music
I get happy at the sight
of Lemnian grapes
getting ripe
(their shoots come early).
And there is the sight
of the swelling of the wild fig.
And when it is ripe
I will pick it and eat it   1320
and praise the trustworthiness
of the gods of the season,
and after tribulation know joy,
and in the summer that follows
swell full like the fruit.

Much better than to have to observe
some captain of the wars,

a man loathsome before the gods,
and three crests to his helmet,
and dressed in a purple   1330
that is harsh to the sight,
and he swears is the true dye of Sardis.
But if he gets to fight in his coat of purple
it will run like the dye of the Cyzicenes.
And he'll be the first to leg it
like some tawny horsecock,
his crests all aflutter.
And me stood there hoping he gets put in the bag.
But when that mafia get home
they do the unendurable,   1340
draw the lots for the campaign lists
and strike off two or three
at the top or the bottom.
And tomorrow they march.
And this poor chap has no grub,
for he was unaware it was needed.
And there he is, stood by Pandion's statue,
and he sees it, realizes what's up,
finds out about this dreadful thing.
That's how they treat us countryfolk.   1350
Those from the town do a bit better
at the hands of these men of godly force
who chuck away their shields.
But they shall give me them to bring to account,
God willing. I owe them a judgment,
these men that play the lion at home
and the fox in battle.

TRYGAEUS
　　Well, well, well, look at all this lot coming in for the wedding
　　　　　　feast.
(produces a helmet crest)
　　Take this and wipe the tables with it.

It's absolutely of no use now.   1360
And bring us in sweetcakes, and thrushes,
and masses of hare, and rolls.
(Enter a procession of tradesmen with such placards as "Peace in our
Time," "Peace and Prosperity," etc.)

SICKLE MAKER
   Where is Trygaeus, where is he?

TRYGAEUS
   I'm stewing thrushes.

SICKLE MAKER
   O my dear, dear Trygaeus, you brought us such blessings
   when you made peace. They wouldn't buy a sickle for free
   and now I get fifty drachmas apiece.
   And my friend here gets three drachmas a cask from the farmers.
   But Trygaeus, accept these sickles,
   and take anything else you want as a gift.   1370
   And please accept this. Out of our proceeds
   from these proceedings, this is our wedding gift.
(A second procession begins to enter, composed of men put out of work by
the arrival of peace. They carry such placards as
"Give us back our jobs," "Down with Spartan
Imperialism," etc. Most are carrying the goods they
cannot sell. They stand in a queue to see Trygaeus.)

TRYGAEUS
   Ok, put them all down, and into the feast
   quick as you can, for the salesman for weapons
   has just arrived, and he's a bit upset.
(Exit first procession.)

CREST MAKER
   You have torn my being from the ground, Trygaeus.
   You have destroyed me.

TRYGAEUS
    What is it, O son of evil? Something wrong with your crests?

CREST MAKER
    You have taken the roof from my head
    and the strength from my limbs—   1380
    and these men also, and the maker of spears.

TRYGAEUS
    So what shall I offer you for your crests?

CREST MAKER
    What will you give?

TRYGAEUS
    What shall I give?
(looks carefully at the helmet crest)
                        This is a bit embarrassing. This definitely
    needs a bit of work. Well, I'd give you
    three quarts of raisins. I can always
    wipe the table with it.

CREST MAKER
    So go and get the raisins.
    That's better than nothing.

TRYGAEUS *(suddenly waving the crest about, so it disintegrates)*
    Chuck them out, chuck them out, rubbish for the crows!   1390
    It's molting! Nothing doing with this crest!
    I would not pay one raisin for it.
(The crest maker stands, head bowed.)

BREASTPLATE SALESMAN
    What shall I do with this breastplate?
    It cost me ten minas to make, and it has such a flame
    to its beauty, and what use is it?

TRYGAEUS

    Oh, you shan't lose anything on that.
    I'm sure I can give you a fair price.
    It's just right to shit in.

BREASTPLATE SALESMAN

    Cease to mock me and my wares!

TRYGAEUS *(having opened out the breastplate)*

    Look, put three stones, like this. And isn't it just right?   1400
(sits on it)

BREASTPLATE SALESMAN

    So wipe yourself, you cannibal!

TRYGAEUS *(getting into remarkable contortions with the breastplate)*

    Like this: put my hand through the bumhole,
    and so . . .

BREASTPLATE SALESMAN

    What 'bout the other one?

TRYGAEUS

    Indeed, by Zeus, you should be careful with an oarhole
    when you've taken the trouble to pinch it from a ship.
(sits pretending to row)

BREASTPLATE SALESMAN

    Will you sit and shit on forty minas' worth of art?

TRYGAEUS

    Indeed, by Zeus, I will, you little shit. Isn't
    the comfort of my anus worth a thousand drachmas?

BREASTPLATE SALESMAN

    Come on, then! Bring on the silver.   1410

TRYGAEUS *(standing up as if in pain)*
> But my dear chap, it nips my bum!
> Take it away: it's no use.
(The breastplate salesman stands, head bowed.)

TRUMPETER *(pushing forward)*
> Now what's the use of my trumpet?
> Though I paid sixty drachmas!

TRYGAEUS
> Well, fill up the bell with lead;
> then insert a rod, and make sure it's long.
> And you'll have just the thing for cottabus.

TRUMPETER
> I am made fun of.

TRYGAEUS
> Another suggestion:
> Put in the lead as I said,   1420
> and suspend a few threads,
> and behold! a perfect scales
> for use in the fields
> to weigh figs for laborers.
(The trumpeter stands there as if he cannot believe it.)

HELMET SALESMAN *(coming forward with despair on his face)*
> O spirit that cannot be appeased, you have destroyed me.
> I paid good money for this, and now what am I to do?
> Who is going to buy it?

TRYGAEUS
> Oh, take a little walk to Egypt
> and sell them over there.
> They're just what they want   1430
> to measure the purge for their bowels.

TRUMPETER *(in despair to the helmet salesman)*
>   O my dear spear seller, how dreadfully we are treated!

TRYGAEUS
>   But he's all right.

HELMET SALESMAN
>   But what am I to do with my helmets?
>   What's the use?

TRYGAEUS
>   Look: stick some handles on, and make cups,
>   and they will sell better than ever.

HELMET SALESMAN
>   Let us depart, spear seller.

TRYGAEUS
>   No need, I really am going
>   to make an offer for his spears.   1440

SPEAR SALESMAN
>   So what's your offer,

TRYGAEUS
>   I'll saw them in two, and use them as vine props:
>   hundred a drachma, that's my offer.

SPEAR SALESMAN
>   We are put down! We must go my friend, we must go away.
>   *(The second procession goes out, making noises of lamentation. Enter two*
>   *small boys.)*

TRYGAEUS
>   By Zeus, here are two little boys come to join us,
>   extra guests who were going to pee, but it will be

enough to sing us a tune to open the feast.
Come and sing by me, my boy, come and stand by me,
and so begin.

FIRST BOY

"Now we begin with the men of the sword!"   1450

TRYGAEUS

Oh shut it about the sword, thrice wicked demon.
In the time of Her peace this is foolish and accursed.

FIRST BOY

"And so they came close, and coming together
thumped leather target and shield boss one on another."

TRYGAEUS

Shields! Why remember shields!

FIRST BOY

"And then mingling of the lamentation and triumph noises of
            men."

TRYGAEUS

For God's sake—"lamentation of men."
Cease by the God of true ecstasy
to speak of men in pain
and the clashing of shields.   1460

FIRST BOY

But what should I sing about?
Tell me what you'd like to hear.

TRYGAEUS

"And so they feasted on the flesh of fine oxen," and all that.
"And they set out the best, and partook of delight."

FIRST BOY

"So they unsaddled their horses, and feasted on the flesh of fine
                    oxen,
for they were weary of war."

TRYGAEUS

Quite right. They were all fed up to the teeth with fighting,
so they had a feast. So tell us what happened after they got fed up
and had something to eat.

FIRST BOY

"Oh they got plastered, and then came to an end."   1470

TRYGAEUS

Ceilings, no doubt.

FIRST SERVANT

"And then they marched forth from the towered city,
and a ceaseless shout arose."

TRYGAEUS

Oh, little boys and battles! You only sing about war,
don't you? Whose kid are you?

FIRST BOY

Me?

TRYGAEUS

Yes you, by Zeus!

FIRST BOY *(very demurely)*

Lamachus' son.

TRYGAEUS

O God!
I did wonder hearing you   1480

if you were not the kid
of someone in love with war,
someone who did not want an armistice.
Get to the warriors, sing to them.
(First boy exits.)
Now where's Cleonymus' son.
(pats the second little boy on the head)
You sing before we go in.
You know enough not to sing
about all the dark and gruesome things.
Your Dad's got his head screwed on!

SECOND BOY

"My shield is giving comfort to my enemy.   1490
I left it in a bush with no blame attached,
for there I threw it against my will."

TRYGAEUS

Tell me, my little squirt,
are you having a dig at your Dad?

SECOND BOY

"But I preserved my life."

TRYGAEUS

You're really one up on your parents, you really are.
But let's go on in. I am quite sure
that you will never forget
your little song about the shield,
being whose son you are.   1500
*(The previous choruses except for the young girls, all now dressed in
                    country clothes, have come on stage in various
                    groups during the recent action. They are now
                    seated at tables brought on during the previous
                    interlude, but not eating. Trygaeus turns to them.)*
Having put off your work and stayed,

you've only got to get stuck in.
I don't expect you'll need conscription.
. Fall on like men! Consume all with your jaws!
For what point is there in white teeth
unless they're up to a little chomping!

CHORUS

Oh, we know that, but thank you for pointing it out.
They still seem rather reluctant to eat.

TRYGAEUS

But you must be hungry, and it's before you.
Attack the hare! Not every day   1510
you meet cake like this in desert ways!
Eat it, or meet the just reward for sin!
(The chorus rises suddenly just in time to meet the bridal procession,
composed of the chorus of young girls and everyone
in the cast not already on stage, coming in dancing
and carrying bridal torches. Trygaeus rushes to the
side of his bride, Opora.)

CHORUS

Now is the time for words of good omen.
Now is the moment for the bridal procession.
Now is the time for the fashioning of torches.
Now we must make merry and dance!

Our gear must go back to the country,
we must carry it back in procession.
We must dance, we must pour libations.
Hyperbolos must be expelled.   1520
But we also pray to the gods
to return resources to the Greeks,
to provide a plenitude of barley
and adequate wine,
and figs to nibble,

and children for our women,
and to summon every blessing back
from the fore-time,
and make an end
to the forging of iron.   1530

TRYGAEUS *(to his bride, with whom he is arm in arm)*
Come my woman: back to the country.
How lovely you are when you are with me,
and lovelier still when we shall lie down.
Hymen! Hymen! Ho!
Hymen! Hymen! Ho!

CHORUS
Thrice blessed to have the blessings
that justly are yours.
Hymen! Hymen! Ho!
Hymen! Hymen! Ho!

SEMICHORUS OF MEN
And what's to be done with her?   1540
What's to be done indeed?

SEMICHORUS OF WOMEN
Bring her to fruit!
Bring her to fruit!

SEMICHORUS OF MEN
And so we raise her up
in orderly proper fashion,
as behooves us men.
(Trygaeus and Opora are raised up on the shoulders of the chorus.)

SEMICHORUS OF WOMEN
Go home in your beauty,
go home with no problem

but to gather your figs.
Hymen! Hymen! Ho!   1550
Hymen! Hymen! Ho!

SEMICHORUS OF MEN
Oh, he is big and he's well made.

SEMICHORUS OF WOMEN
And she is sweet as any fig.

TRYGAEUS
And you shall say,
as you feast and get merry,

CHORUS
Hymen! Hymen! HI HO!
Hymen! Hymen! HI HO!

TRYGAEUS
Rejoice, rejoice,
all that are here,
and enter with me   1560
to eat of good cakes.

Celebrating Ladies

Translated by
David R. Slavitt

Translator's Preface

The idea of doing a version of the *Thesmophoriazusae* was both attractive and daunting to me. This is the only translation I have undertaken of a text where Dudley Fitts, my teacher at Andover, had previously ventured.[1] What temerity to presume to do what he had done!

There are extenuating circumstances, however, the most salient of which is that I'm not seventeen, as I was when I sat in his classroom in Bullfinch Hall forty-five years ago. I'm older now than he was then. And I'm alive while he isn't. These considerations meant that my attempts at Aristophanes' patter would give me the chance to have a kind of conversation with Fitts—I could not only ask myself, as I often do, how he might have solved a particular problem but could go, if I chose, and look up what he actually did.

My method of working, however, was to keep his book on the shelf. Enough time had elapsed since my last reading of it that I had forgotten most of its details. I decided that the most useful and at the same time the most intimate connection I could devise would be to consult it only later, after I was done. That would be time enough in which to see how close we were, where he'd come out better, where I'd been particularly clever, and, more important, whether, in a gross way, I could suppose he might have approved of what I'd produced.

The hardest part was the title itself. As he points out in his introductory note, "The unwieldy title is even more awkward in translation, for we should have to say something like 'The Women Keep the Thesmophorian Festival,' which is clear enough but not particularly stimulating." His solution was "Ladies' Day," which is not at all bad. What could I do to match that? "Celebrating Ladies" with its noun as either subject or object of the participle is syntactically ambiguous, and the phrase, therefore, has a pleasing shimmer. I prefer it and, just as important, I believe that Fitts would

---

1. Dudley Fitts, *Ladies' Day* (New York: Harcourt Brace, 1959).

have been amused. He was a demanding teacher, but a generous one who invested himself in his pupils and who could delight in our achievements.

Robert Fitzgerald had been one of those pupils in Fitts' early days at Choate. I came along rather later, but when I met Fitzgerald—some years after Fitts' death—and told him that I, too, had been one of Fitts' boys, his face lit up and he said to me with great heartiness, "That makes us brothers."

As Fitts says of the piece,

> It is one of the three plays—the others being *Lysistrata* and *The Women's Parliament* (*Ecclesiazusae*)—in which Aristophanes handles the idea of women interfering in men's affairs, and this may be a reason why the comedy did not take first prize at the Dionysia [of 411 B.C.]. Another reason may be the fact that so much of the play is literary parody. There is action enough: some of the rough-&-tumble is as hearty as anything in the comic theatre; but it must be confessed that an extended burlesque of any poet, even a Euripides, lacks popular appeal. Nonetheless there is great vigor here, of a heady kind, and even this special kind of fun has overtones that reach us across the centuries. (p. vii)

My own impulse would be to let the play speak for itself, as it does quite well. If it is "important," that's because it is funny. But Fitts does not disdain the schoolmaster's information students may need to show off with when they write their papers, and if he gives it, I suppose I should, too. Or, better yet, I repeat his own words:

> The play is a friendly attack upon Euripides. (Another and minor poet, Agathôn, is less amiably handled in the Prologue, but it is Euripides who is the principal butt.) Why Euripides? First of all, because he was a shock: his innovations outraged authority and threatened the established conventions of the tragic stage, and his iconoclastic treatment of religious and social questions had already identified him with the new science, the new philosophy. Euripides, like Ibsen, was one of those germinal artists who both enchant men and make them think. Artists of this kind are never welcomed by the guardians of social order. An

aristocrat and conservative—and Aristophanes was both—will distrust them instinctively. Add the petty but exacerbating flames of literary intrigues, the interminable cliquish squabblings of writers and artists among themselves, and you have reason enough for an attack upon Euripides. The wonder is that it is so good-humored; for while it is true that the dramatist takes a merciless drubbing at the hands of Aristophanes, it is also true that the very magnitude of the attack, the documentation itself, must be accounted a compliment of the most flattering kind. Such brilliant parody implies admiration, however qualified that admiration may be. (pp. viii–ix)

That, too, seems to me not at all bad. And having written that phrase a second time, I remember that it was a part of Fitzgerald's grading system at Harvard. It was a demanding scale he'd picked up from his association with Fitts. In ascending order, there were these possible notations on one's paper: PB (for "pretty bad"), NTB ("not too bad"), NB ("not bad"), and, if one had really done splendidly, NAAB ("not at all bad").

Good? That never came into it, except perhaps as the ideal toward which we all, pupils and teachers, ought continually to strive.

Cast

MNESILOCHUS
EURIPIDES
SERVANT to Agathon
AGATHON
CHORUS of celebrating ladies
FIRST SPEAKER
SECOND SPEAKER
MRS. CLEONYMUS
MICA
CRITYLLA
CLEISTHENES
PRYTANIS
SCYTHIAN SERGEANT
MAGISTRATE
POLICEMAN
NONSPEAKING
    Stagehands
    Thratta, Thracian maidservant
    Sergeant
    Soldiers
    Dancing girl
    Flute-girl
    Various servants and attendants

(*On a street in Athens in front of Agathon's house, two elderly men
are walking together. One is Euripides, the tragedian; the other is
Mnesilochus, his brother-in-law.*)

MNESILOCHUS
    How long O Lord? Are we there yet? We've been tramping
            around
    since dawn, and my wind is giving out, and my feet, too.
    Where are you taking me, Euripides?

EURIPIDES

You wouldn't believe your ears! Wait till you see.

MNESILOCHUS

See with my ears? You must be pulling my leg.

EURIPIDES

No, no. The shoe is on the other foot.

MNESILOCHUS

Foot? Ear? What are you talking about.

EURIPIDES *(lyrically)*

See here. Hear, here! You see? It's all matter of taste.
They're different senses, but they all make the same sense.

MNESILOCHUS

Or the same nonsense.   10

EURIPIDES

I'll explain it to you. Cosmogony recapitulates ontology.
Aether is all around us, and all living creatures
breathed and moved and swam in the aether. She gave us
sight in our eyes, and hearing in our ears.
But it's all the same world they see. You hear?

MNESILOCHUS

Thank you very much. I am delighted
to be enlightened so, and by so eminent a poet.

EURIPIDES

My pleasure. Think nothing of it.

MNESILOCHUS

I promise you, absolutely. My mind is almost as numb
as my feet. You're a poet: you know all about feet, right?   20
Mine are killing me.

EURIPIDES

Come over here and listen.

MNESILOCHUS

Yes, by all means.

EURIPIDES

You see that gate?

MNESILOCHUS

See it, hear it, taste it.

EURIPIDES

Be still!

MNESILOCHUS

You want the gate to be still?

EURIPIDES

Just listen!

MNESILOCHUS

You want the gate to listen? You want me to listen to a gate?

EURIPIDES

Inside that gate dwells Agathon, the famous, the noble,
the eminent tragic poet.

MNESILOCHUS

Agathon? Never heard of him.

EURIPIDES

Agathon? You've never heard of Agathon?

MNESILOCHUS

A dark, heavy-set fellow?

EURIPIDES

No, not at all.

MNESILOCHUS

A bushy red beard?

EURIPIDES

No! But surely, you know him?   30

MNESILOCHUS

No. I don't think so. I've never laid eyes on him.

EURIPIDES

Then you're keeping your eyes closed these days down at the
        bath-house.
But look, that's his servant approaching. Him with the kit
for a sacrificial offering—the myrtle branches and the pan of
        coals.
His master has sent him to pray, no doubt for inspiration.
*(Agathon's servant enters from the house. Euripides and Mnesilochus
        draw back a little.)*

SERVANT *(making a general announcement to the public)*
Let's keep it down here. A little quiet, please,
a little respect. Genius at work. The muses
are shy and don't like noise and riot.
Quiet, everyone. No ifs, ands, or excuses.
Let the aether be unruffled   40
and every footfall muffled.
Let the waves as they break on shore
omit their customary roar . . .

MNESILOCHUS

Bombast and bullshit!

EURIPIDES
> Didn't you hear him? Hush now!

SERVANT
> Birdies up in the sky, please do not tweet, *Bird stop*
> And down on the ground, mousies, watch your feet.
> Don't stomp and shuffle. The poet
> is working . . .

MNESILOCHUS
> > Oh, go stow it!

SERVANT
> My master, Agathon,   50
> can't work with these carryings-on.
> I beg you, sirs, he is now about to . . .

MNESILOCHUS
> About to what? Fart? Throw us a big moon? Take a leak from the
> > roof?

SERVANT *(unable to ignore them any longer)*
> I beg your pardon, sir? What is this?

MNESILOCHUS
> We are the aether, forgetting to be unruffled.

SERVANT
> I was about to say that he is about to lay . . .

MNESILOCHUS
> An egg? A chicken? A sheep?

SERVANT
> The foundation of a brand new play.
> An epigram here, a rejoinder there,
> a joke he has somehow pulled out of the air.   60

A touch of wisdom, a dollop of fun,
something appealing for everyone.
He makes the language jump and dance . . .

MNESILOCHUS

And to top it all off, pulls down his pants!

SERVANT

And what ill-bred louts have we here, at our very threshold?

MNESILOCHUS

I wouldn't hold your thresh if you paid me! I wouldn't touch it
with a ten-foot pole—not even if I had a ten-foot pole.
The verse your master purveys is perverse. And his prose is
worse.

SERVANT

In your prime, you may have been a pederast and a rapist,
and now in your dotage you are reduced to pissing in the street   70
and making a public nuisance of yourself. How sad!

EURIPIDES

Pay him no mind, but call our your master for me. I pray you,
sir . . .

SERVANT

No need for prayers. He is coming directly.
He likes to walk when he is composing choral odes,
letting the sun warm his lines to make them supple.
(*Servant exits, going back into the house.*)

MNESILOCHUS

Why are we here? What am I supposed to do?

EURIPIDES

Just keep quiet and watch and listen.
Ah but soft, through yonder window breaks the son-of-a-bitch
himself.

MNESILOCHUS

> I don't understand. What are you so nervous about?
> Come on, spill it. I'm your brother-in-law, after all.   80
> We're family. You can tell me what the trouble is.

EURIPIDES

> I'm in the soup he's cooked up. And I could drown.

MNESILOCHUS

> What soup? Can't you ever talk in intelligible sentences?

EURIPIDES

> This day decides whether Euripides shall live or die.

MNESILOCHUS

> I hear, but I don't see. Or the other way around. Could you
>   give me
> a teeny hint? The courts don't sit today. No Council meets.
> It's the middle day of the Thesmophorian Festival.

EURIPIDES

> That's it. Bingo! This is the day all the women meet
> in the temple where the number on their card
> is mine. They'll cook my goose. And settle my hash.   90

MNESILOCHUS

> A bizarre dish. Why would they want to do that?

EURIPIDES

> The feminists claim I'm not treating them fairly.
> They're sick of what they call my male-chauvinist bullshit!

MNESILOCHUS

> All bullshit is male, I'd think. But what do you care what they
>   say?
> And what does that have to do with our being *here*? I still don't
>   see it.

EURIPIDES

    Here's my plan. My stratagem. The plot. The donnée as it were
of the action, the *inventio* . . .
(Mnesilochus sighs wearily.)
                           All right, here's the deal.
I will get Agathon, the tragedian—the dramaturge and
monument of the theater, don't you know?—
to dress up as a women and go to their meeting.

MNESILOCHUS

                                What on earth for? 100

EURIPIDES

    He'll find out what they're saying and what they're planning to do.
He might even speak up for me, a few well-chosen words.

MNESILOCHUS

    That's your idea? In drag, he'll speak up for you? In falsetto?

EURIPIDES

    Precisely.

MNESILOCHUS *(sarcastically)*

        What a nifty idea. A really astonishing plan!

EURIPIDES

    I like it.

MNESILOCHUS

      But, but . . .

EURIPIDES

              Quiet, here he comes.
*(The door of the house opens and Agathon is wheeled out on a miniature
stage. He is got up as Dionysus, and his costume is
a unisex tunic.)*

MNESILOCHUS
    Here he comes? Where? Where is he?

EURIPIDES
                                                    There.
    In that piece of theatrical equipment.

MNESILOCHUS
                                        I must be going blind.
    I don't see any man. That's . . . Madonna, maybe?

ambiguous

EURIPIDES
    No, but be quiet. He—or she or it—seems to be about to sing.

MNESILOCHUS
    Grunge rock? Gangsta rap? I can't imagine!   110

AGATHON (*as an actor doing Dionysus, very campily and mannered*)
    Oh dear, O death,
    it simply takes away my breath,
    to think of all the pretty ladies
    laid in the ground and gone to Hades.
(*now answering himself, as the chorus*)
    Truly, truly, what you say
    resounds in all our hearts today,
    freeborn maidens, proud to be
    attendants of Persephone,
    so sweet and kind. And even sweeter,
    is her mother, dear Demeter.   120
(*again as actor*)
    Come, you Muses, bless Apollo,
    such a sunny pleasant fella,
    patron of the a cappella
    song. I dedicate my solo
    piece to him whom I admire
    and to his truth I pluck my lyre.
(*as chorus*)

switching lining actor for the chorus? always your purge?

Whether it be by skill or luck, or
plain hard work, each humble plucker
hopes his notes will somehow rise
from earth to the immortals' skies.   130

MNESILOCHUS

Isn't he just ravishing! It touches the heart.
It touches the rest of me too. He's a musical massage parlor.
(addressing Agathon)
Sir? Madame? In the words of the immortal Aeschylus,
"I am struck a deadly blow and deep within." Who are you?
What are you? And why are you gotten up that way?
I can't figure out your costume. Are you a transvestite
or simply a deranged person?

AGATHON

Why good sir, as Aeschylus also says, "Sticks and stones
will break my bones, but words will never hurt me."
I choose my garb to suit my poetic needs. A poet, sir,   140
must be prepared to do anything for the furtherance of his art.
When I write about a woman, I have to think and feel
as a woman would, I have to become a woman,
or at least dress up as a woman, and think womanly thoughts.

MNESILOCHUS *(aside, to Euripides)*

He's kidding, isn't he? You never tricked yourself out like that
when you were writing *Phaedra*, did you?

AGATHON

When I write as a man, I get myself dressed as a man,
for the soul is apt to follow the body's promptings.

MNESILOCHUS *(again to Euripides)*

And when you wrote *The Cyclops*, that satyr play,
did it ever cross your mind to put out one eye?   150

AGATHON

    A poet, I say, ought to be as smooth as his poems.
    Not rough and bushy. And poets should dress themselves
    in garments with flowing lines, in silk pajamas,
    or elaborate brocades of Tibetan lamas.
    Think of Anacreon or Alcaeus in boots
    and blue jeans, looking like rude brutes.
    Or think of Ibycus or Phrynicus the fair,
    who liked to wreathe wildflowers in his hair.
    They looked good, and they wrote good poems too,
    for what you are determines what comes from you.   160

MNESILOCHUS

    It's crazy, but he's half-way right. I mean,
    the opposite is true. Philocles is awkward
    and lame, and so are his plays. And Xenocles is ugly,
    and so is his work. Theognis is a cold fish,
    and everything he does seems cold and fishy to me.

AGATHON

    That is why I get myself up a little. To get myself up . . . for
             writing.

MNESILOCHUS

    That's what you call getting it up?

EURIPIDES

    Leave him alone. I was like that when I was starting out.

MNESILOCHUS

    In what prep school was this?

EURIPIDES *(to Agathon)*

    Sir, if I may have your attention for just a moment?   170

AGATHON

    Yes, sir.

EURIPIDES

        Agathon, I won't beat around the bush,
which is not a good thing to do, causing blindness
and other forms of debility. I shall come straight to the point.
I have a favor to ask of you.

AGATHON

                          Ask away.

EURIPIDES

        Today is the day the ladies are celebrating
their festival. They are all going to get together
to trash me, to get back at me for what they say
are the anti-feminist anti-heroines in my plays.

AGATHON

        I am sorry to hear that. But what can I do?

EURIPIDES

        Why everything. What I want is for you to disguise yourself   180
as a woman—which, obviously, you're able to do—
and go there and take your place among them and listen,
and even speak in my behalf. Who else but you
could be as eloquent as I would be, myself?

AGATHON

        But why don't you go yourself?

EURIPIDES

                      They all know me.
And I have a gray beard, which very few women
are sporting these days. You've got that nice round face
as smooth as a baby's ass, and a high-pitched voice
that sounds not unlike a woman. You move like a woman . . .

AGATHON

        Euripides, hold on there a minute.

EURIPIDES

                                  Did I forget something?   190

AGATHON

    Yes, your own words in your own play. Remember, in *Alcestis*,
    the father asks Admetus: "You value life;
    what makes you think I don't?"

EURIPIDES

                            So? What about it?

AGATHON

    It wasn't just something the actors say. It has a kind of truth to it.
    There's a hell of a risk one takes trying to sneak into that ladies'
                assembly.
    It's your problem. It ought to be your risk. You must bear your
                burden,
    close your eyes, and take whatever comes.
    Take it like a man!

MNESILOCHUS

                Take what like what man? You are happy to take it
    wherever you can find it. For you it's fun.
    For him, it's just an enormous pain in the ass.   200

EURIPIDES

    What is it that you're afraid of, Agathon?

AGATHON

    They'll hurt me! They'll do to me worse than what they'd do
                to you.

EURIPIDES

    Why would they do that?

AGATHON

                   I'm too much like a woman already.
    They'd think I've really and truly decided to change gender.

MNESILOCHUS
I see what you mean. He's right.

EURIPIDES
You mean . . . you won't do it?

AGATHON
No, I won't.

EURIPIDES
I'm done for. Screwed, blued, and tattooed.

MNESILOCHUS
Don't despair. There must be some other way . . .

EURIPIDES
What can I do?

MNESILOCHUS
To begin with, you can tell Agathon to go fuck himself.
You've still got me as your faithful friend and in-law!

EURIPIDES
I do? That's right, I do!
(The penny drops. He decides to send Mnesilochus instead.)
Well, that's just wonderful. That's terrific. 210
That's fine and dandy. First, you have to take off the coat.
(in the sing-song manner of the old Smith and Dale routine)
Take off the coat. Take off the coat.

MNESILOCHUS *(mystified, but removing his coat)*
There, the coat is off. Now what?

EURIPIDES
It's a close shave!

MNESILOCHUS

What is?

EURIPIDES

What I'm going to give you.

MNESILOCHUS

What? A shave? Here in the street?

EURIPIDES

Yes.

MNESILOCHUS

No!

EURIPIDES

What about it, faithful buddy? Chum? Pal? In-law?

MNESILOCHUS

You're out of your mind, but you're right. I did promise.

EURIPIDES *(to Agathon)*

You've always got a razor with you, Agathon. Lend me one.

AGATHON *(producing a case of razors)*

Pick any one you like.

EURIPIDES

Excellent! Admirable. I am deeply obliged.

(to Mnesilochus)

Okay, sit right down. Puff out your cheek, would you?

(Mnesilochus does so. Euripides shaves off one side of his beard.)

MNESILOCHUS

Ouch! What are you, crazy?

EURIPIDES

Quiet. Sit, sit, sit. Don't move   220
or I'll have to tie you down, the way they do
when they shave crazy people.

MNESILOCHUS *(struggling, getting up out of the chair, and moving away)*
I'm crazy?
You're crazy! You're completely out of your mind!

EURIPIDES
And where do you think you're going?

MNESILOCHUS
To a temple for sanctuary. You're going to hack me to death.
I swear by Mother Demeter . . .

EURIPIDES
You're going to look very odd that way
with one cheek shaved and the other not.

MNESILOCHUS

I don't care!

EURIPIDES
Come on back. Remember your promise . . .

MNESILOCHUS *(returning to the seat)*

I'm doing a very stupid thing.

EURIPIDES *(resuming the shaving)*
That's right. Raise your chin just a little. A little to the left . . .   230
Very good. But stop wriggling.

MNESILOCHUS

Oh, ah, ouch! Oooh!

EURIPIDES
> There we are! All done.

MNESILOCHUS
> > And I look like a plucked chicken.
> Or a plucked chicken-hawk.

EURIPIDES *(producing a mirror and holding it up for Mnesilochus)*
> > I think you look just fine.
> Here, take a peek! See?

MNESILOCHUS
> > I look like . . . Michael Jackson.

EURIPIDES *(lighting a match)*
> And now, we singe the hair.

MNESILOCHUS
> > Or a cooked chicken. What are you doing?

EURIPIDES
> Just a little singe, for smoothness.

MNESILOCHUS
> > You're setting me on fire.
> You're burning me alive! Help, help! Fire!
> Fetch us a bucket. Or a chamber pot.

EURIPIDES
> A chamber pot?

MNESILOCHUS
> > You're scaring the shit out of me.

EURIPIDES
> What an bundle of nerves you are. It's all right. It's finished.   240

MNESILOCHUS

You mean I'm finished. Usually they wait for the death
before they cremate you. I'm a cinder.

EURIPIDES

Here's a sponge. I'll just wipe you off.

MNESILOCHUS

At both ends, if you please.

EURIPIDES

Don't be gross!
(to Agathon)
You won't help out in person, but perhaps you could oblige us
by lending us one of your spare frocks? A nice dress and a sash?
You have, I'm sure, an entire closetful of that kind of thing.

AGATHON

Anything you like. Help yourselves.

EURIPIDES

Something in silk, perhaps?
This yellow one is nice. What do you think?
Slip into this, why don't you?
A vision for sure!

MNESILOCHUS

It's Aphrodite's nightie!

EURIPIDES

It wants to be tighter.   250

MNESILOCHUS

Where's the sash?

EURIPIDES

Here it is.

MNESILOCHUS *(getting into the spirit of this)*
    It should hang nicely around the legs, shouldn't it?

EURIPIDES
    Just lovely! And now a little cloche, and a hairnet . . .

AGATHON
                                                    Like this?
    This is one of my personal favorites.

EURIPIDES
                                    I'll just bet it is!

MNESILOCHUS
    How do I look?

EURIPIDES
                    Good enough to eat. Or to be eaten.
    An outer cloak, I think.

AGATHON
                        There's a pile on the couch. Pick one out.

EURIPIDES
    And pumps. Not too high-heeled.

AGATHON *(offering his own)*
                            Like the ones I'm wearing?

MNESILOCHUS
    A fashion statement, or what?

AGATHON
    It's a look. No question about it. I've done what I could,
    and if someone would be kind enough to wheel me back in?   260
(Stagehands come and take him away.)

EURIPIDES *(to the audience)*
Doesn't he look like the Woman of the Year?
(to Mnesilochus)
The look is good. But remember, if you're going to speak,
try to do it in a high girlish voice.

MNESILOCHUS *(giggling and speaking in falsetto)*
I'll certainly do my very best!

EURIPIDES
Okay, then. You're on your way. And good luck to you.

MNESILOCHUS *(not in falsetto)*
Wait a minute. Hold on there . . . First, I need your promise . . .

EURIPIDES
What promise? What are you talking about.

MNESILOCHUS
That if this turns out badly, you'll stand by me.
This is your crazy idea, after all.

EURIPIDES
I promise. I swear!
By every god there is. All for one and one for all!

MNESILOCHUS
You mean, "All for one and you are he."   270

EURIPIDES
What do you want from me? I promised, didn't I?

MNESILOCHUS
Cross your heart and hope to die or stick a needle in your eye?

EURIPIDES

Oh, go on. Go, already! There's the signal on top of the temple
roof.

It's about to start. Hurry, you'll be late.

(Euripides and Mnesilochus exit. The background curtain opens to reveal
the Temple of the Thesmophoria. Mnesilochus
reenters, accompanied by Thratta, a Thracian
maidservant who carries a basket on her head.)

MNESILOCHUS *(in falsetto)*

That's it, Thratta, that's a good girl. Hurry along.
Look at all those burning torches. We're going to have one hot
time
at this Thesmophorian whoop-de-doo!

(aside)

I do hope we get away with this.

(again to Thratta)

Now set down your basket, dear. Where are the little cakes,
the offering we're making to the two goddesses? Hand them over,   280
and I'll pass them along to Demeter and Persephone.

(He takes the cakes and puts them on an altar. The next two lines, an
entirely sincere prayer, are in normal voice. Then
he resumes in falsetto.)

O you great goddesses, be nice to me today,
and let me get away from here without any broken bones.
    And may my daughter find herself a nice husband,
wealthy enough and stupid enough. And may her little brother
our dear little Bubba turn out to be a little less of a dope
than we have always had good and sufficient reason to suppose.

(to Thratta)

Now where do you think would be a good place for me
to hear the speeches? You don't have to stay. Who knows
what they're going to be talking about? It may not be what   290
I want my little jewel of a maid to hear. You'd better go on home.
There must be some dusting to do . . . Or go polish the silver.

(Thratta exits as the Chorus of celebrating ladies enters.)

FIRST CHORISTER

    Hear, ye! Hear, ye! Silent be,
    and pray to the double deity,
    mother Demeter and her child
    Persephone—for they have smiled
    on us and blessed us all our lives
    as daughters, mothers, and as wives,
    given us wealth and wit and beauty,
    and taught us how to do our duty   300
    to gods of earth and sky. Now we
    assemble here in harmony
    to discuss among ourselves the great
    issues that face the Athenian state.

SECOND CHORISTER

    Grant that our discussions now
    be wise and useful and allow
    the commonwealth of women to
    succeed in what we try to do—
    as we combine here to defend our
    rights and those of all our gender.   310

CHORUS

    Sing Paean, Paean, hey, hey, hey,
    Radcliffe, Wellesley, all the way.
    Mt. Holyoke, Barnard, Smith, Bryn Mawr,
    all bless what we are fighting for!

FIRST CHORISTER

    Apollo, hear our prayers, and Zeus!
    We will not tolerate abuse.
    as the League of Women Voters meets
    in conclave and we take our seats.
    In the oceans, full of fish,
    let Poseidon hear our wish,   320
    as in the woods Athena, too,

blesses what we're here to do.
Let Oreads on mountain peaks
hear each woman as she speaks,
and Nereids beneath the wave
assist, approve of our conclave.
Strike the gong and pluck the zither,
for the women who have traveled hither,
free and noble matrons all.
Assembled in this ancient hall,   330
we invoke you, deities,
and hope our fervent prayers may please
and prompt your help now in our fight
to win the day and take back the night.

SECOND CHORISTER

O gods and goddesses, you who dwell
on Olympus' top, and you, as well,
the Pythian, Delian, and all others,
and their sisters and their mothers,
listen to us assembled here
and teach our enemies to fear   340
our righteous anger. Curse the lives
of men who do not love their wives,
adore their mothers as they ought, or
dote as they should upon each daughter.

CHORUS

Oh, yes, oh, yes, and let us rehearse
the list of all those whom we curse:
(*severally*)
I curse whoever opposes our assembly of women.
I curse whoever wants to restore tyranny or make himself tyrant.
I curse the Persians and the Medes.
I curse Euripides.   350
I curse servants who betray their mistresses to their masters.
I curse go-betweens who fail to deliver messages to lovers.

I curse rich old ladies who steal men away from us with
      expensive presents.
I curse lovers who break their promises.
I curse women who take presents from men but then won't put
      out.
I curse bartenders who water their drinks.
(together)
    Let them all rot in hell,
    them and their families as well.
    And may the gods whom we're addressing
    shower down on us their blessing.   360

SECOND CHORISTER
    We pray the gods to grant our prayers,
    for our sakes and those of our heirs.
    Help our deliberations, teach
    us wisdom in our thought and speech.
    Likewise, bring woe and pain to those
    who, breaking their sworn oaths, expose
    the secrets we keep here to foes,
    betraying their friends and sisters to
    men who would frustrate what we do
    to improve our lives and make our city   370
    strong and safe and clean and pretty!

FIRST CHORISTER
    Oyez, oyez! Hear ye, hear ye! The Planning Board
    of the Women's National League for Peace and Freedom
    is now in plenary session, having been called to order
    at the motion of sister Sostrata, endorsed and seconded
    by President Timocleia and Recording Secretary Lysilla.
    The first item on the agenda, is the question of what to do
    with—or should I say to?—the so-called tragedian, Euripides.
    I think we are agreed that he's guilty. All we have to decide
    is what the appropriate punishment ought to be.   380
    The meeting is open . . . Who wants to speak first?

FIRST SPEAKER

I do.

FIRST CHORISTER

If you would, put on the speaker's diadem.

(to the assembly)

Order, order. Silence, please. Let us show our sister here
some courtesy and give her our undivided attention.

(to the speaker)

Are you ready dear? Don't be nervous. Take a deep breath
and remember that you're talking to friends. It's just that
there are a lot of us here in the room with you. Okay?

FIRST SPEAKER

This is very intimidating. I never thought I'd be getting up here
to stand at the rostrum and speak to you all. But . . . but I just
had to do it.
And the reason is that I'm angry. Really furious deep down inside 390
at the way that Euripides insults us and scoffs at us and makes
fun of us.
Who does he think he is? A greengrocer's son! A nobody. A
nothing!
But he insults us every chance he gets, accuses us of all kinds of
sins,
puts us up on the stage as demonstrations of every vice you can
think of—
He calls us liars, and cheats, and faithless, and drunks, and
gossips,
and he says we're rotten to the core, a misery to mankind, a
plague.
What do you think happens then? What do you suppose he
intends?
The men leave the theater and come back to us, and they're
looking in closets
and checking under the bed for lovers, and measuring how much
wine is left

in the barrels, and . . . It's just terrible, that's what it is. You're
        sitting there   400
minding your own business and doing some needlework, and he
        thinks
What's she prettying herself up for? For me? For someone else? Who
        else?
You're clearing the table and you drop a plate, which can happen
        to anyone,
and he figures your mind is somewhere else, or with someone
        else,
and you're just counting the minutes until you can get free and
        go meet this
stud you're so hot for, you're dropping the dishes on the floor. I
        mean, really!
Until Euripides came along, everything was fine and our
        husbands trusted
and loved us, but now they suspect us . . . Having babies, for
        instance.
You can get hurt, you know? You can goddamn die! It's
        dangerous!
So if you decide to avoid the entire thing, and go out to hire
        someone else   410
to do the actual labor, by which I mean, just go out and buy a
        baby,
it's not so easy anymore, now that they're poking and feeling
and prodding the pillow you're wearing to pretend you're
        pregnant.
They even want to be there at the delivery, want to sit right there
        on the bed
and see with their own eyes that enormous head pop out! As if!
There's no confidence any more, no assumption of common
        decency
and good will. Old guys with money are suspicious about the
        motives
of young girls, because Euripides says we're just out for their
        drachmas,
and he has got them all worried that we're going to be shrews

and make their lives a living hell. That's not a good attitude!   420
And I ask you, how many of you are finding that your husbands
        now
are locking you up in the house when they leave, and buying
        watchdogs,
huge Molossian mastiffs, to bark and scare away the most ardent
        admirer.
Is that a way to be? Is that how we're supposed to live? And they
        count things,
count the silver, check the wheat, look at the stores of wine and
        oil and olives,
mark the containers, and act like bookkeepers and accountants,
so that you can't skim anything out of the household money
        anymore
to buy yourselves the presents that they ought to be bringing you
        and don't
because they haven't thought of it for years and have been taking
        you for granted.
You used to be able to do these things easily enough, but no
        longer,   430
now that Euripides has been telling them and warning them and
        turning them
against us . . . It has got to stop. It's hopeless now, and Euripides
        has got to go!
He's poisoned their minds against us, and I say it's time for us to
        poison him.
So that's what I move. That Euripides be poisoned. I'll write it
        out
and give it to the recording secretary in proper form so we can
        put it to a vote.
Thank you all very much for your attention. I really appreciate it!
(sits down)

FIRST CHORISTER
    That was very good. Very well done! Wasn't she just fine, ladies?
    What a well-made speech. It's not so hard after all, once you get
        up here.

It's even kind of fun. Thoughts come into your mind and words
pop out of your mouth, and it's just the way it ought to be. A
          great speech!   440
I'm sure we're all proud of her. Who in all Athens is more
          eloquent?
What man is there who can get up and talk as well as we do?
If Xenocles himself were to get up here, he couldn't do a whit
          better,
and he's beaten Euripides three times now—or is it four—in the
          contests.
We'd just hoot him off the platform! Now, who's next?

SECOND SPEAKER

Ladies, I have only a couple of things to add to what the previous
          speaker
said here so well just a moment ago. But I want to tell my own
          personal story,
and share with you all how Euripides has hurt me. I work for a
          living.
It's not a great living, but I get by and support myself and my five
          children,
because I'm a widow, you see, and what else is there for me to
          do?   450
Anyway, I weave myrtle wreaths for offerings to the gods. And
          Euripides
is telling people that there aren't any gods. Well, you can see what
          that does!
That kind of irreverent remark can really ruin my business. And
          it has.
My grosses are down by half this quarter compared with a year
          ago.
And if people don't start buying wreaths again, I can't see how it
          will improve
in the near term or ever. So I add my voice, whatever it's worth,
and I say kill him. He's a nasty little twerp and he deserves it.
I'm going to leave my ballot here with the recording secretary
          and get back

because somebody's got to mind the shop, and we have our
>
> orders to fill . . .

There are still a few pious people left in the world, thank the
>
> gods!   460

And those dear children of mine have to be provided for. So,
>
> thanks a lot!

(leaves)

FIRST CHORISTER

Wasn't that special? Wasn't that just wonderful? I am so happy to
>
> see this,

and to hear my sisters getting up and talking with logic and
>
> reason and all

about the important issues of the day that are facing us in these
>
> difficult times.

When we get together like this, we can see just how powerful we
>
> are

and we can bring about important social and political change
>
> here in Athens

that will make the whole world sit up and take notice. And I
>
> ought to add

that I agree entirely with what's been said. I think Euripides is
>
> a bum

and that Athens and all of Greece would be better off without
>
> him

and without his annoying, irreverent, and generally smart-ass
>
> remarks.   470

(Mnesilochus comes to the lectern.)

MNESILOCHUS

Madam Chairperson, ladies, and . . . ladies!

I want to endorse every word that has been spoken here so far.

I agree with it all. And I understand entirely why you are so
>
> angry

at this Euripides person because of what he has been saying about
>
> us.

I hate him myself. Like poison. You bet. He is, I swear

on the heads of my babies, the most exasperating man.
But let's be honest, here. I mean, can we talk?
There's nobody here but us girls, after all. And just among
          ourselves,
let's admit that a lot of what he's been saying is simply the truth,
that he's found us out, and got our number, and there's a hell of
          a lot   480
he hasn't said and maybe doesn't even know about. Am I right?
Or am I right? Which of us doesn't have a disgraceful story
she'd rather not have him re-enacting on some stage. I can think
          of a few . . .
But let me tell you just one, about how, when I'd just been
          married
for three days, I played a dirty trick on my poor little hubby
who was fast asleep in the bed next to me, snoring and farting
          the way they do.
I heard my lover—he and I had been getting it on since we were
          little kids together—
scratching and tapping at the outer door, just the way he'd done
when I was still living with my parents. So I get up and start to
          tippy-toe out of the bedroom
and downstairs. And he asks me where I think I'm going.   490
I tell him I have a cramp and need to go to the outhouse, and he
          tells me
juniper and sage is good for that and keeps the bowels moving
          right along.
I call back to thank him for this information while I'm pouring
          water
on the door hinges so they won't squeak when I open the door.
          Which I do
and sneak out to meet him on the corner at Apollo's pillar, set up
          out there
to honor the god of the streets. And I lean against that pole and
          hold on
for dear life while my old beau rams his pole into me from
          behind, doggy style.

Euripides doesn't have anything like that in any of his plays, does
        he?
And the stories I've heard about some of us whose tricks have
        been wilder
and cleverer than any of mine—lovers smuggled in with the
        laundry or out   500
with the trash, quick boffs with the milkman or the postman or
        the plumber,
handing out the nookie to one and all while hubby is sitting ten
        feet away
in the breakfast nook stirring his coffee and reading the paper
        and smiling
like the moron he is. I've heard of wives out all night who come
        creeping in
at dawn, the stink of sex with a dozen different men reeking from
        every orifice,
and they chew garlic in order to hide it from the old bozo until
        they can bathe.
So Euripides says uncomplimentary things about Phaedra? Fuck
        Phaedra, I say.
Let him write whatever he wants about her. She's a harmless
        myth.
Meanwhile, you know and I know that there are women who
        spend ten days
in their charade of accouchement while their servants are out
        negotiating   510
to buy an infant. And the dopey husband is running from one
        quack to another
for whatever drugs might help his poor suffering missus in her
        time of trial.
And he comes back about five minutes after they've smuggled
        the basket in
with the kid, with a gag on its mouth to keep it from making any
        noise,
and the wife asks the husband to step outside, and they unwrap
        the brat

and then present it to him—it's maybe a week old, and he's
        astonished
at what a prodigious child it is, another Heracles, a super-infant,
        a demi-god.
"Oh, and it looks just like you," the lady says, "don't you think?"
        And the dope
beams and nods and agrees with her, and says what a lucky guy
        he is. Is it true?
We do these things, right? You all know it. We women are not so
        much   520
sinned against, I say, as we are, ourselves, the criminals and
        sinners.

FIRST CHORISTER
    This is not quite the line of argument we had been expecting.
    Who is this person? Where does she come from? Does anyone
        know her?

SECOND CHORISTER
    I cannot believe that during her harangue, no one was objecting.
    These are vile accusations she makes against us, lower and lower.

THIRD CHORISTER
    Under any rock, you'll find some scorpion willing to sting you
        with his so-called truth!
    But I can't believe my ears! That someone should speak this way
        just isn't couth.

FIRST CHORISTER
    There's nothing in all the world, I think, so bad as a shameless
        shrew,
    a woman like her—except maybe another one of us. But what
        can you do?

FIRST CHORISTER
    Order! Let us have order here! We are agreed I think that this
        can't stand   530

and that something must be done to this impertinent person. I
    suggest . . .
something terrible, something utterly dreadful, something that
    really hurts:
I propose that we strip her clothes off her and give her a bikini
    waxing.

MNESILOCHUS

What? What is this? I thought the rules were that anybody could
    say
whatever she wanted, and that there would be free speech by free
    women
with liberty and justice for all, and . . . What good is freedom if
    it's only to say
what everybody in the room approves and agrees with anyway?

FIRST CHORISTER

What you were doing here isn't liberty but license. This is over
    the top
and beyond the pale, and . . . How dare you speak on behalf of
    Euripides,
who is a terrible influence . . . He is always criticizing us and
    never praising,   540
Phaedra he gives us and Medea. But how about Penelope?
    Wouldn't that be amazing?

MNESILOCHUS

It would be, because there are lots of Phaedras and Medeas and
    Melanippes but not so many Penelopes around
    these days. I haven't heard of any, anyway!

FIRST CHORISTER

You are insufferable! You get worse and worse! Are you out of
    your head?
This is slander and libel and insult . . .

MNESILOCHUS

                                        And every single word I've said
        is the truth and you know it! Indeed, the real truth is
                        considerably worse,
        as I can prove beyond a shadow of a doubt, citing page, chapter,
                        and verse.
        Doing the hubby's dishes with the toilet brush? You think you're
                        so clever!
        Stealing the best funeral meats to give your procurer and blaming
                        the dog?
        Or the women who murder their husbands that we are forever
        reading about? Or slipping them aphrodisiacs that drive them
                        nuts? How about that?   550

SECOND CHORISTER
        This can't go on. This is offensive, outrageous . . .

MNESILOCHUS

                                        Only because it's true.
        As it was true about the girl who buried her father alive . . .

FIRST CHORISTER
        Stop! Stop this at once!

MNESILOCHUS

                                Or the women who switch babies,
        passing off the maid's sons as their own and giving away
        their own daughters to grow up with the servants?

SECOND CHORISTER

                        By Demeter and Persephone, I swear
        I'll make you eat those words. I'll . . . I'll . . . I'll pull your hair!

MNESILOCHUS
        Hen-fight! Hen-fight! Come on, now and we'll see
        who's mistress around here—you, you bitch, or me!

SECOND CHORISTER

You want to fight? We'll fight!
(*She hands her outer cloak to one of the other women.*)
Hold this for me, would you?

(*to Mnesilochus*)

All right, now, you harridan, you hussy, you douche-bag,   560
I'm going to beat your enormous lardy ass black and blue . . .

FIRST CHORISTER

Wait a minute, ladies, hold on. I see somebody coming,
running, as if she had some important news. Before you two
tear into each other, let's find out what it is she has to say.
(*Enter Cleisthenes, heavily made up and in bizarre dress but not in drag.*
He wears a pacifier on a ribbon around his neck.)

CLEISTHENES

No, no, it's me, Cleisthenes, your pal, your so to speak
bosom buddy . . . No ladies' man exactly, but as lady-*ish*,
as lady-ish as they come, if you get my drift.
But I come with a warning. There are rumors going around.
Those little birdies that tell you things are singing,
twittering their heads off everywhere,   570
and I wanted to let you know of the danger you're in.

FIRST CHORISTER

What danger? What are you talking about, sweet cheeks?

CLEISTHENES

They say that Euripides is up to no good
and has sent his brother-in-law, a nasty man,
to spy on you all and report what you've talked about
at your private meeting here.

SECOND CHORISTER

But how could he do that?

CLEISTHENES
    Euripides has shaved his hair off and singed him
    and got him up in a woman's dress.

MNESILOCHUS
                            Oh, no!
    I don't believe it. Nothing like that could have happened.
    What man would let himself be shaved and tweezered   580
    and singed like that? The humiliation! The pain!

CLEISTHENES
    Honor bright! I had this on the best authority.

FIRST CHORISTER
    We must clear this up. We'll find him out. If he's here,
    we'll find him, you can bet on that. What nerve!
    What a low and evil thing! But it's not surprising.
    Will you give us ladies a hand and help us conduct
    our search? It could be fun!

CLEISTHENES
                            Yes, I can see that.
    (addressing one of the women)
        And who are you, madam?

MNESILOCHUS *(aside)*
                            Where can I hide?

MRS. CLEONYMUS
    Who? Me?

CLEISTHENES
                    Yes, you!
    (aside)
                            I get to grope them!
    This is my lucky day?

MRS. CLEONYMUS

          I am Cleonymus' wife.   590

CLEISTHENES

    Does anyone know her? Is she telling the truth?

FIRST CHORISTER

    Oh, yes. We all know her.

CLEISTHENES *(to a woman beside her with a baby)*

          And who is this with the baby?

MRS. CLEONYMUS

    She's my nursemaid.

MNESILOCHUS *(aside)*

          Here he comes! I'm dead meat.

(desperate, as he tries to tiptoe away)

    The loo? The little girls' room? Does anyone know where it is?

CLEISTHENES

    Wait! Stop her! Who's that pussy footing away?

FIRST CHORISTER *(aside, to Cleisthenes)*

    I have no idea who she is. Except that she's weird.

CLEISTHENES *(to Mnesilochus)*

    One moment, there, madam . . . You are?

MNESILOCHUS

          Off to pee?

CLEISTHENES *(detaining her by grabbing her sleeve)*

    Hang on. Just hold your water for a moment.

MNESILOCHUS

I beg your pardon. Let me go. It's . . . the Crimson
Tide. I have a gym excuse.   600

CLEISTHENES

Not bloody likely.
What's your husband's name.

MNESILOCHUS

My husband?

CLEISTHENES

The man you married!

MNESILOCHUS *(truly desperate)*

Oh, him. Of course. From the Piraeus.
Anonymous! The writer? Surely, you've heard of him.

CLEISTHENES

Anonymous?

MNESILOCHUS

Sure, the son of . . . Pseudonymous! Also of the Piraeus.

CLEISTHENES

You're pulling my chain!

MNESILOCHUS

Oh, I wouldn't do that.
Not for all the world. I swear!

CLEISTHENES

Have you ever been
to the Thesmophoria before?

MNESILOCHUS

Oh, yes, of course.

CLEISTHENES
When?

MNESILOCHUS
Before. The other time. Actually, often.

CLEISTHENES
And who was your bunk-mate last year?

MNESILOCHUS
A dark-haired girl, she was.
I remember she had . . . a Greek name . . .

CLEISTHENES
This is ridiculous!   610

FIRST CHORISTER *(to Cleisthenes)*
Let me ask her a couple of questions. About last year's rites.
No man is allowed to know these things. Would you give us a
moment
(Cleisthenes moves away a few steps and allows the first chorister to interrogate Mnesilochus.)
Now tell me, if you can, on the first day, last year,
what was it we did?

Interrogation (lighting)

MNESILOCHUS
On the first day? We did . . . what we always do.
We . . . drank?

FIRST CHORISTER
Yes, that's right. And on the second day?

MNESILOCHUS
On the second day? We . . . drank?

FIRST CHORISTER
You're just guessing now,
aren't you. But what about the third day?

MNESILOCHUS

                                        The third day?
And then we really got smashed. Oh, boy! We got totally wasted!
Xenylla pissed herself, and . . .

FIRST CHORISTER

                                No! Nonsense! You're the one.
Cleisthenes, this is the one. He's a man!   620
The one you warned us about.

CLEISTHENES

                            You think so?

FIRST CHORISTER

                                        Yes,
but it's easy to prove one way or another. Strip him!

MNESILOCHUS
Strip? Me? The mother of nine little babies?

CLEISTHENES
Show us what you've got! Undo your sash!

FIRST CHORISTER
He's built like a man. And he doesn't have breasts like ours.

MNESILOCHUS
I'm barren. I never was able to have any children.

→ Flat

FIRST CHORISTER
What about those nine brats you just made up?
What happened to them?

CLEISTHENES

                        He's a man. Just as I said!

FIRST CHORISTER
That's why you said those dreadful things. That's why
you spoke for Euripides, that son of a bitch.   630
And you're another!

CLEISTHENES *(groping Mnesilochus' crotch)*
                              I think I've found his wee one.
It was hiding.
*(First chorister goes around behind Mnesilochus and gropes his
                    backside.)*

FIRST CHORISTER
                    That's what it is, all right. It's small,
but it's there. Or it was. It's gone now.

CLEISTHENES
                                        It's back in front.

MNESILOCHUS
How does one maintain a degree of poise
in such a circumstance?

FIRST CHORISTER
                          We've got you now.

CLEISTHENES
Watch him. Don't let him get away. I'll go
as quick as I can to fetch the constabulary.
(Cleisthenes exits.)

FIRST CHORISTER
Okay, ladies, let us look
in every cranny and tiny nook,
checking every hiding place   640
for any unfamiliar face.

In the closets and the hallways
let us be diligent as always.
Look in the statuary niches
for other intruding sons of bitches.

SECOND CHORISTER
Look with magnifying glasses.
Grope their breasts and pat their asses.
Exercising every care,
inspect what's in their underwear.
Check for whiskers. Feel their muscles.   650
Do they have falsies on? Or bustles?
Hermaphrodite, transvestite, queer?
We want no man intruding here.

THIRD CHORISTER
We will find them out and hurt
that man who hides in a woman's skirt.
From any such blaspheming sinner,
suave old queen or green beginner,
we shall defend ourselves with fury.
Prosecutors, judges, jury,
we shall be executioners too.   660
All other men, when we have done
our worst with these we've caught, will run
in fear of us and the gods. These guys
will learn what should be done to spies.
(While this is happening, Mnesilochus, in desperation, tries a new tactic,
snatching the baby of Mica, one of the women; she
pursues him.)

MICA
Help! Stop him! Hey, you! Help. He's got my baby. Come back.
He grabbed my little baby, just pulled him away from me. Get
    him!
Stop him, somebody. But don't hurt the child. Help!

MNESILOCHUS

> That's right. Don't hurt the child. And don't make me hurt the
> > child.
>
> Or, to make it even clearer, don't make me hurt the hostage. You
> > see?
>
> I don't get hurt? He doesn't get hurt. But if you try to mess with
> > me,   670
>
> I rip this kid limb from limb, like a chicken on a carving platter.
> I'll put him on the altar and offer him up as a sacrifice to the
> > gods,
>
> and you can watch as the sacrificial knife plunges into his baby
> > fat.

MICA

> Oh, help me, help me, somebody. This is too terrible. O sisters,
> > help!
>
> Do something. Save my little treasure. Don't let that monster
> > hurt him.

FIRST CHORISTER

> This is dreadful. This is vile.

SECOND CHORISTER

> He's stolen that poor woman's child!

THIRD CHORISTER

> He's shameless and his heart is black!

FOURTH CHORISTER

> Give her little baby back!

FIRST CHORISTER

> What do you think you are doing, sir?   680

MNESILOCHUS *(indicating the bereft mother)*

> Making a spokeswoman out of her!
> An advocate and ally who
> will help me escape from all of you.

MICA

    Give him whatever he wants, I say.

SECOND CHORISTER

    You mean, we should let him get away?
    Somewhere we have to draw the line,
(*aside*)
    but I'm glad that baby isn't mine.
(*again, to the women*)
    The law can't be ignored. We must
    impose a punishment that's just
    and fair, and cruelly amusing   690
    to us whom he has been abusing.
    Young girls, misses, madams, dames,
    let us cast him into the flames.
    Bring the kindling. Pile it high.
    This son of a bitch is about to die!

FIRST CHORISTER

    Get sticks and branches. Let this rude
    impostor here be barbecued!
(*During the foregoing, Mnesilochus has been unwrapping the swaddled
        baby, which, as it turns out, isn't a baby at all, but
        a wineskin!*)

MNESILOCHUS

    Ah, baby, baby. We are dead ducks. Our goose is cooked. Our
                chicken is charbroiled,
    but we're in this together, you and me, right? And for you they'll
                feel some
    charity, some pity, some . . .
                        Out-fucking-rageous! These women will be   700
    the death of me! This is no a baby. It's . . . adult refreshments!
(*takes a sip*)
    Not bad, not bad. A nice nose, and not too much oak . . .

FIRST WOMAN *(to one of the other women)*
>That's it, pile up the faggots there—
(to the other's look of incomprehension)
>>it means sticks of kindling.

MNESILOCHUS
>That's right. Pile up the faggots, whatever they are.
(to the bereaved mother)
>And this is really your own little pride and joy?

MICA *(not yet knowing that he knows her secret)*
>Absolutely. My own flesh and blood, I swear.

MNESILOCHUS
>I suppose you can offer me its proof. Your dear little half-pint.
>More like a liter, actually. How old . . . ? What vintage was your
>>dear one?

MICA
>Just a tiny tot!

MNESILOCHUS *(holding up the wine flask)*
>>Some healthy tot you have here, madam.

MICA
>Give it back. Hide it at least!

MNESILOCHUS
>>Some chance of that!   710

MICA *(quietly, to Mnesilochus alone)*
>They'll burn you! I'll help them, I swear.

MNESILOCHUS
>I'll take your little bundle of joy with me!

MICA *(louder and for public consumption)*
　　Spare my child. Take me instead . . .

MNESILOCHUS *(aside)*
　　Mother-love and sacrifice! It's right out of Stella Dallas.
　　But it's no use. My heart is not broken, or even dented.

MICA
　　Spare my child!
(quietly)
　　　　　　　What are you going to do with it, you pig? It's mine!

MNESILOCHUS *(taking a swig and then producing a knife)*
　　I am going to sacrifice your wee one, here. I am going to cut the
　　　　　　　little bugger's
　　belly open and pour out his blood as a libation to the gods.
*(He slashes the wineskin and it empties out onto the ground. Mica tries
　　　　　　　to catch what handfuls of wine she can and lap
　　　　　　　them up.)*

MICA
　　You are lower than whale shit, you are. What a mean thing to do!

MNESILOCHUS
　　You may have the lifeless cadaver to do with what you will.　　720

MICA
　　What earthly use is this?

MNESILOCHUS
　　　　　　　My feeling exactly!
(Enter Critylla.)

CRITYLLA
　　Mica! What's happened? Someone has napped your kid? That's a
　　　　　　　bummer!

MICA

    This pissant here is the villain. Don't you let him get away.
    I'm going for the cops. Cleisthenes and I will settle his souvlaki.

MNESILOCHUS *(to the audience)*

    What now? What am I to do in this crisis? If this were a play,
    I'd know. The clever playwright would have figured out
    some amazing piece of business that, in the real world,
    wouldn't have a prayer of working out . . . But what would it be?
    What would my brother-in-law devise to get one of his stage
            heroes
    out of the impossible fix of the second act curtain?
(pauses)

                                  Any suggestions?   730
    Come on, you've all read Euripides, right? No? Not even the *Cliffs*
            Notes?
(pauses)

    How about . . . How about the *Palamedes*? Doesn't ring any bells?
    Well, the thing is that Palamedes was put to death at Troy,
    and his brother Oeax—that's O, E, A, X if you're taking notes—
            sends the news
    to their father in Euboea by writing out the message on oar
            blades that he throws
    into the sea, and they float on home, don't you know . . . ?
    Well, it's a dopey idea, I admit, but has any of you got a better
            one?
(pauses)

    No? So okay. But there are no oar blades here. Only these votary
            tablets.
    Can't have a Thesmophorian festival without the old votary
            tablets now, can you?
    They'll do as well as the oar blades. Pencil? Pen? Stylus? Magic
            Marker?   740
(checks in his pockets and produces a piece of yellow chalk)

    Now what should I write? "Help" is as good as anything else. It
            has a certain

elegance, an admirable brevity, that hint of panic and desperation
    we want . . .
(*writing*)
    H E L P
(*He does this several times on cardboard votary tablets and flings them
    out into the auditorium.*)
    Euripides, help! Come quick!
    Euripides? This had better work!
    Euripides! Come here, I need you.
(*pauses, then, directly to the audience*)
    Euripides is a jerk.
    This is the most lame-brained idea I've ever heard of.
    And these women, I am afraid, are going to be very unpleasant
        to me
    very soon unless I get help very fast.   750
(*retires to stage left with Critylla guarding him*)

FIRST CHORISTER
    Okay? You done now? It's our turn? Good!
    Because we women, too, want to be admired and understood,
    and appreciated, even, which we will be one of these days,
    even though you'd never think so, judging by Euripides' very
        depressing plays.
    "A woman's a two-face, a worrysome thing that'll leave you to
        sing the blues
    in the night." Yes, yes, we all know that, and it isn't exactly news,
    but if it were true, why would men be running after us all the
        time and devoting their lives
    to getting us to live with them and be their lovers and mistresses,
        and sometimes even wives.
    And when they've got us married, they want us to stay in the
        house and cook and clean,
    because they're afraid if we go outside, we might see better
        looking possibilities, and also be seen,   760
    and they're jealous and crazy and all the rest of it. What sense
        does that make

if we're such worrysome things, such catastrophes, and such
              torments, for gods' sake?
Possessive and complaining at the same time? It tells you
              something about women maybe, but more about
              men,
who don't have the courage of their convictions, and are screwed
              up seven ways to Thursday and then
some. I mean, if one of us goes out to visit a friend—a lady
              friend, that is—and decides to spend the night,
the husband, who has been complaining about her, goes crazy
              with jealousy mixed with worry. It is, I tell you,
              quite
ridiculous. Women are not like that. Women are better than
              men. It's clearly true.
Look at the terrible things that men are always doing and that no
              woman would ever do.
We don't march armies off to war and then lose. We don't set sail
              in our expensively outfitted armadas
to get our asses whipped, in battles off Tyre, for instance, but
              that's what happens to our husbands and . . .
              faddas (?).   770
Victory, however, is a female goddess, to whom these unlucky
              admirals and generals pray
as they go into battle, not having any idea what they're doing but
              hoping that this will be their lucky day.
We don't do politics or high finance, and none of us practices
              law. We don't get up and make speeches
we know are misleading. We are not filling our bellies at the
              public trough. We are not pigs. We are not
              leeches.
Go to the post office and look at the wanted posters, and read
              about one criminal after another,
and notice, if you please, that they're all members of the
              masculine gender. You don't see anyone's sister
              or mother
with her mug-shot up on the wall there. Not that we're perfect,
              but your typical woman's crime

is borrowing some of her husband's loose change off the top of
    the bureau, which we plan to repay sometime.

SECOND CHORISTER

Now it's my turn, and I get to do the strophe,
to say how women are not thieves and murderers, thuggish and
        oaf-y,   780
and we don't burgle or mug people, and wreck the environment,
or drink up or piss away our inheritances and then wonder
        where they went.
We are kind and thrifty, modest and loving, virtuous and sweet,
while men are so many crocks of shit, nasty bastards who aren't
        good enough to lick our feet.

THIRD CHORISTER

And this part that I'm doing here is the epirrhema, whatever the
        hell that means,
and I'm here to tell you that even with those few good things
        men do, there's usually a woman behind the
        scenes,
supporting and encouraging, and listening, and helping in all
        kinds of ways,
and soothing you guys when you fall down and skin your knees,
        and lavishing love and praise
when you do something right, as from time to time, even the
        dumbest and laziest and most shiftless of you
        may.
But do we get any share of the credit, any of the glory or fame,
        not to mention a reasonable share of the pay?   790
You hear me, you louts and morons out there, you understand
        what those of us up here say?
You're squirming, as you should, because it's the truth and you
        know it. All right. Now we can go back to the
        play.
(Chorus marches off. The lights go up on Mnesilochus and Critylla.)

MNESILOCHUS

No sign of him. That stupid idea
from the *Palamedes* didn't work.
Maybe he just doesn't like that play anymore.
I can understand that. But I've got to do something,
or these women are going to be extremely unpleasant.
Ah, how about something from his new piece?
Helen is at least rational in what it assumes.
And I *am* dressed up in women's clothing—so I can do Helen.   800

CRITYLLA

What's with you, motor-mouth? What are you muttering there?
Who is this Helen you're talking about? Helen Damnation!
You just keep your lip buttoned until the cops come.
You understand me?

MNESILOCHUS *(as Helen)*

Is this the face that stopped a thousand launches?
We are in Egypt, and you must imagine here the Nile,
perilous with asp and alligator—or is it the crocodile?
I am the moon and Menelaus is the sun.
Actually, he's my husband, or one of them, anyway.
Tyndareus was my father . . .   810

CRITYLLA

Your father? Your father was Curly Stooge!

MNESILOCHUS

And I am Helen.

CRITYLLA

Still doing female impersonations? You have a slow learning
curve.

MNESILOCHUS

Men bled for me on the banks of the Scamander.

CRITYLLA

Menstrual envy, I have no doubt.

MNESILOCHUS

                                    I try to be patient

waiting for Menelaus . . .

CRITYLLA

            You bet men'll lay us. But not men with high standards.

MNESILOCHUS

Why does my life drag out so, day after day?

CRITYLLA

Because the crows that are waiting to peck you to death
aren't yet hungry enough.

MNESILOCHUS

                        But soft, through yonder windows,
something, something . . . Dare I hope? Is it he?
(Enter Euripides as Menelaus.)

EURIPIDES

To what great king does this impressive palace   820
appertain? And does he entertain
strangers whom the billowy wave has tossed
upon his sandy strand?

MNESILOCHUS

            This is Proteus' palace.

EURIPIDES

And what did I have him say here? Proteus says . . .

CRITYLLA

You guys are nuts, you know that? And who is this Pretty-ass?

EURIPIDES

Oh, yes! I have it. "What is this shore where the wind
has driven our fragile barque?"

MNESILOCHUS

Egypt-land!

EURIPIDES

A camel lot. How far we are from home!

CRITYLLA

This isn't Egypt. This is Demeter's Temple.

EURIPIDES

And Proteus is at present here in these parts?   830

CRITYLLA

An ass and pretty parts? The long sea-voyage
has addled your wits. You'd think these intellectuals
would know more . . .

EURIPIDES

He is no more!
Alack! Oh dismal day! Where is his tomb.

MNESILOCHUS

I'm sitting on it.

CRITYLLA

This is no tomb? This
is a temple, remember? Hello? Anybody home?

EURIPIDES

And tell me, stranger, why do you sit here, veiled
and full of grief.

MNESILOCHUS
They want to marry me off
to one of Proteus' sons.

CRITYLLA
You're off your nut!
(to Euripides)
Nobody wants to marry him. He's a prankster   840
who dressed himself up as a woman and slipped in among us
to rob us, I guess. Or else he's some kind of pervert.

MNESILOCHUS *(to Critylla)*
Go on, insult me. Calumniate away. See if I care.

EURIPIDES
Tell me, O stranger, who is this dreadful woman
who abuses you so?

MNESILOCHUS
Theonoe, Proteus' daughter.

CRITYLLA
I am not, either. I'm Critylla, Atitheus' daughter,
of the Gargettus district. I know my own name!
And I know yours, too: you're mud.

MNESILOCHUS
You're pleading is all in vain. I shall never marry,
and certainly not your brother. I shall keep faith   850
with Menelaus, my husband, who fights at Troy . . .

EURIPIDES
What have you said? Oh, let me see your face!

MNESILOCHUS
I blush to let you behold this grief-worn visage.

EURIPIDES

    I cannot speak! My heart is overflowing.
    Can it be? Do I dare to hope? What is your name?

MNESILOCHUS

    My name? What's yours? I too am all a-twit.

EURIPIDES

    Tell me at least whether you be Greek or Egyptian.

MNESILOCHUS

    Greek! Or even, to drop a hint, Hellenic.

EURIPIDES

    Are you indeed Helen herself? Yourself?

MNESILOCHUS

    And you must be . . . Let me guess! Menelaus?   860

EURIPIDES

    Indeed, you behold that miserable person.

MNESILOCHUS

    Oh, after so long, come to my longing arms!
    Take me away. Let us begone, together.
    Give me your kisses. I am your Mrs.
    Take me away, away, today.

(Euripides starts to lead Mnesilochus offstage, but Critylla realizes that
        the exit is not altogether play-acting.)

CRITYLLA

    Hey, just a goll darn minute there. Where do you two clowns
    think you're going? Another step and I whip you!

EURIPIDES

    Let go of my wife. This is the woman I love!
    I am taking her home to Sparta, where she and I
    will reign as king and queen and live happily ever after.   870

CRITYLLA

In a pig's pizzazza you are. He's a crook and you're another.
And here is the magistrate coming to decide what to do with
         him,
accompanied, I see, by his Scythian enforcer.

EURIPIDES

That is, I believe, my exit cue.

MNESILOCHUS

You're going off and leaving me here? You bastard!
What do I do now?

EURIPIDES

                  Just hold your horses.
I'll be back. I'll think of something. I promise.
I'm a playwright, remember. I'm good at this kind of thing.

MNESILOCHUS

I see how good you are. I'm still here, aren't I?
*(Enter Prytanis, accompanied by a Scythian archer, a sergeant of the
         guard, who carries a whip, a bow and arrow-
         quiver, and a short sword. There are also some
         supernumerary soldiers who accompany the
         sergeant and will help in carrying Mnesilochus.)*

PRYTANIS

Sergeant, this is the perp Cleisthenes told us about.   880
(to Mnesilochus)
And a sorry looking piece of human detritus you are.
(to the sergeant)
Take him inside there and . . . tie him onto a plank.
Then bring him back out here and watch him.
Don't let anyone come close to him. If anybody tries,
use your whip. You got that?

MNESILOCHUS
                              Excuse me, your honor?
May I make one request? As a suppliant, I hold out my hand
to yours—which is usually filled, I know, with gifts of silver and
                gold—
to entreat you. Your worship? Your excellency? Sir?

PRYTANIS
    What do you want?

MNESILOCHUS
    Don't let them stake me out in these women's clothes.   890
    Tell the Scythian sergeant to strip me naked.
    It's bad enough to be spread-eagled out in public
    for passersby to laugh at, but . . . not in drag!
    Even the crows that peck at me will laugh.

PRYTANIS
    No. Just as you are. That's what the court
    decided. Silks and satins and buttons and bows.
    Suffer. And let the people be entertained.

MNESILOCHUS *(to audience)*
    What a revolting development this is.
    In buttons and bows, yet. Can it get any worse than this?
*(All the actors leave the stage. The chorus comes on to perform the
                ceremony of celebration.)*

FIRST CHORISTER
    Let us dance and celebrate   900
    in proper form the mysteries
    of the goddesses, the great
    mother and daughter whom we please
    by doing as we do on these
    occasions. At a dizzying rate,
    whirl to the music's harmonies

and let each lady consecrate
herself to these divinities.

On this day of solemnities,
poor starving people have a reas-   910
on not to eat: no bread, no cheese.
(interrupting herself and abandoning rhyme)
    Does the fact that they fast most of the time make them holier
                        than us?
    Or less holy, because their stomachs are smaller and they feel it
                less?
    I wonder about that, sometimes.
    Don't you ever wonder about things like that? No?

CHORUS
    Let the chorus likewise sing
    and praise the gods in everything.
    Because we are women, do not think
    we'll bad-mouth men, although they stink.

    The point is here to celebrate   920
    our own refinements, which are great.

    See how beautiful we are,
    as we dance here to the strummed guitar.

    Apollo, Diana, Hermes, Hera,
    Pan and the Graces all draw nearer

    and smile to hear us sing this way.
    Women are wonderful. This is our day.

    Keep good time and let the skies
    respond to our songs with admiring sighs.

    Let Bacchus, ivy-crowned, approve   930
    how we sing and how we move.

And Dionysus, the theater's patron,
bless each maiden and each matron.

Anàssa katà, kalò kalà
yay, yay, yay, Nikè!
Bryn Mawr!

And let the nymphs of Cithaeron say,
as all of us do who are here today,

yay, yay, yay, Nikè!
Bryn Mawr!   940
(The chorus traipses off. The Scythian sergeant comes in with his soldiers,
            who carry Mnesilochus spread-eagled on a plank.
            The soldiers exit.) *Rolling on*

SCYTHIAN SERGEANT *(speaks with a heavy foreign accent and in a*
            Chinese/Swedish sing-song)
You be staying outside here, by yumping yimini, I think.

MNESILOCHUS
Sergeant, please . . .

SCYTHIAN SERGEANT
            You be wasting your breath.   *Bring Brute.*

MNESILOCHUS
At least loosen the straps a little.

SCYTHIAN SERGEANT
            Ah, si, bueno. Yavohl.

MNESILOCHUS
You are making them tighter.

SCYTHIAN SERGEANT
            You like-um dat?

MNESILOCHUS
    Oh! Oh no. What kind of an accent is that?

SCYTHIAN SERGEANT
                                I am an Auslander.

MNESILOCHUS
    From Ausland?

SCYTHIAN SERGEANT
            Ich bin ein Barbarian. Zehr politicàlischer incorrecto.
    You be shutting up now. Me be fetching a chair. More better, no?
    You can see me comfy-like? You suffer more.
(Sergeant departs to get himself a chair.)

MNESILOCHUS
    What fun that brother-in-law of mine has arranged for me!
    What a pain he is! But wait, I see him. Oh, great Zeus! There is
            hope yet.   950
    Here he comes, old trusty Euripides . . . And he is got up like . . .
(Euripides, on a crane, flies across the stage, costumed as Perseus.)
    Perseus! I get it. The winged sandals, right? So that makes me
    Andromeda. Chained to a rock? You figure that out? Good
            for you!
    And he's coming to rescue me, just like in the play!

EURIPIDES *(as Perseus, singing)*
    O you nymphs and virgins dear,
    I've worked out how to come quite near
    my friend, while that barbarian fool
    is offstage looking for a stool.

    Echo, you who reigns in the caves,
    let me skim above the waves   960
    to help Andromeda my wife,
    and, like a hero, save her life.
(He disappears on the other side of the stage.)

MNESILOCHUS *(as Andromeda)*

    Oh, I am undone. I am the most unfortunate of women.

    A bad person has chained me here, and now a worse one,

    this Scythian loony, is guarding me, while I am exposed

    to the eyes and the laughter of scoffers and the pecking of crows.

    What will become of me? Oh, I am alone and friendless.

    Sing no hymeneal song for me, O ladies,

    but a dirge of grief, some melancholy threne.

    See how I suffer, gods in heaven? And you,   970

    the shades in Hades, look at my torments here.

    Tartarus himself must weep at my plight.

(as himself)

    But where has he gone now? Disappeared again?

    That son of a bitch shaved me, got me dressed up,

    and sent me into this den of lionesses. Now

    where is he? This is a hell of a fix!

(as Andromeda)

                     Oh, evil fate!

    I am accursed. The best I can hope for now

    is a bolt of Zeus' lightning to end this torture.

    There is nothing left in this sublunary world

    to help me now. The shortest path to Hades   980

    is all I ask for. Quick, clean, and painless.

(In the following scene Euripides, from off stage, impersonates Echo.)

EURIPIDES

    Hail, dear maiden. As for your father, Cepheus,

    he who has exposed you on this rock, may the gods

    annihilate him.

MNESILOCHUS

          And who the hell is he now?

EURIPIDES

    I am Echo, the nymph who repeats what she hears.

    In Euripides' play, I appear at this very juncture

    to help the hero rescue the beautiful maiden.

Whatever you say, I will also say. Express
your grief and I will offer my witty descant.

MNESILOCHUS
You will repeat my words?

EURIPIDES

That's the idea.   990

MNESILOCHUS
O Night, divine! how slowly thy chariot rumbles
across thy starry vault in the realms of the Air
and mighty Olympus.

EURIPIDES

A nightie, Olympus.

MNESILOCHUS
Why must Andromeda suffer such woe for her portion?

EURIPIDES

Woeful abortion.

MNESILOCHUS
A sad death!

EURIPIDES

Bad breath!

MNESILOCHUS

You're getting tedious.

EURIPIDES
Getting hideous.

MNESILOCHUS

Oh! knock it off. It's a dumb trick.

EURIPIDES

A bum prick.

MNESILOCHUS
This is getting boring.

EURIPIDES

This is Herman Göring.

MNESILOCHUS
Go fuck yourself!

EURIPIDES *(after a brief pause)*
Go fuck yourself!

MNESILOCHUS
I got you there, didn't I!

EURIPIDES *(after another pause)*
Go fuck yourself!

MNESILOCHUS
A man! A plan. A canal. Panama.

EURIPIDES

A man! A plan. A canal . . . Suez?   1000

MNESILOCHUS
Three smart fellows, they felt smart!

EURIPIDES
Three smart fellows, they smelt fart . . .
(Mnesilochus laughs. Euripides laughs. The Scythian sergeant reenters, carrying a stool. He sits down.)

MNESILOCHUS
So you're back, you son of a bitch!

EURIPIDES

                     You son of a bitch!

SCYTHIAN SERGEANT *(startled)*
    What? What's that? Who's there?

EURIPIDES

                 Who's where?

SCYTHIAN SERGEANT
    This is nicht gut. I go call for help.

EURIPIDES

                 Call for help!

SCYTHIAN SERGEANT
    Quelquechose is phony here!

EURIPIDES

              Funny here!

SCYTHIAN SERGEANT
    Who dat? Who dat?

EURIPIDES

            Who dat?

SCYTHIAN SERGEANT
    Who dat said dat last "Who dat?" Questa cosa?

EURIPIDES

                      Cosa nostra!

SCYTHIAN SERGEANT
    Achtung!

EURIPIDES
>   Mao Tse-Tung!

SCYTHIAN SERGEANT *(to Mnesilochus)*
>   You mock me?

EURIPIDES
>   Vos machts du?   1010

MNESILOCHUS
>   No, it's the woman, behind you.

EURIPIDES
>   A woman's behind? Who?

SCYTHIAN SERGEANT
>   Dove é cette bimbette? Hey, she gone off . . .

EURIPIDES
>   She's a *gonif.*

SCYTHIAN SERGEANT
>   I catch her, you betcha.

EURIPIDES
>   Catcha betcha? Bocce ball!

SCYTHIAN SERGEANT
>   You be shutting your yap.

EURIPIDES
>   Yap, yap, yap!

SCYTHIAN SERGEANT
>   Cut that shit.

EURIPIDES

Shoot that cat.

(*leaves*)

SCYTHIAN SERGEANT (*to audience*)

Ain't this a fuckin' pain in the tuchus!

(*Euripides now enters, costumed as Perseus.*)

EURIPIDES

O heavenly gods! To what land have I come? I am
Perseus! With my winged feet, I tread
the plains of the air, as I carry the Gorgon's head
back home to Argos.

SCYTHIAN SERGEANT

What you jibbering?   1020
Who's ahead?

EURIPIDES

The head of the Gorgon, you Zulu.

SCYTHIAN SERGEANT

Gorgonzulu? That's a big cheese, no?

EURIPIDES (*as Perseus*)

But what do I behold? A young maiden,
beautiful as a god, chained here to this rock
like a boat tied up at a mooring?

MNESILOCHUS

Take pity on me, O stranger! I am so unhappy
and distraught! Also uncomfortable. Free me from these bonds.

SCYTHIAN SERGEANT

You be shutting up now. I betcha after they kill you
you still keep talking. You got a mouth on you
more busier than any whore I ever see.   1030

EURIPIDES
>Oh! virgin! I feel the bite of those cruel chains you wear.

SCYTHIAN SERGEANT
>Virgin? This old cocksucker? You gots to be kidding!

EURIPIDES
>No, no, you buffoon. This is Andromeda, the daughter of
>Cepheus.

SCYTHIAN SERGEANT *(lifting up Mnesilochus' robe)*
>Your daughter of Cepheus has some big dick.

EURIPIDES
>By your leave, I will approach this dear young girl.
>For every man, there is a woman who is his destiny.
>I am aflame with love for this sweet maiden.

SCYTHIAN SERGEANT
>You want him? You got him. His rectile orifice
>is turned your way. You go ahead, make rumpy-pumpy.

EURIPIDES
>Let me untie her and join her on our soft bridal couch.   1040

SCYTHIAN SERGEANT
>No need to untie her. Him. It. You can bore through the plank,
>and stick it in through there. But watch out for splinters.
>*(giggles)*

EURIPIDES
>No, I will untie his bonds.

SCYTHIAN SERGEANT
>   He's in the stocks. You leave his bonds alone.

EURIPIDES

    I'm not afraid of you.

SCYTHIAN SERGEANT

               I cut you fuckin' head off, you scuzz-ball.

EURIPIDES

    What to do? What to do. You can't reason with a mob,
    even if it has only one person in it. All our cleverness
    is lost on this nitwit. How tedious! Let us invent
    some new stratagem better suited to his coarse nature.
(He departs.)

SCYTHIAN SERGEANT *(to audience)*

    He fool with me, I fool with him. You can't fuck a fucker.

MNESILOCHUS

    Ah! Perseus! Don't forget me now. You'll come back? Please!   1050

SCYTHIAN SERGEANT

    One more word, I whipa you candy-ass.
(The sergeant arranges the stool near a wall, sits down, leans against the
               wall, and promptly falls asleep. The chorus enters.)

FIRST CHORISTER

    And now for something completely different. I present to you,
           ladies and gentlemen, for your entertainment
           and delight, the Choral Interlude!
(Two of the choristers step forward and produce batons, which they
           commence to twirl, one at stage left and one at
           stage right.)

CHORUS *(heavily accented, as for a football cheer)*

    Protectress of Athens, I call on thee!
    Be a good goddess. Listen to me.
    You keep the city in your hand,

and we all love you. You are grand.
Boom chicka boom. Boom chicka boom.
Boom chicka ricka chicka. Boom, boom, boom.

Goddess show your lovely face
on our rites in this holy place.   1060
Don't let any men come near
these sacred orgies we have here.
Boom chicka boom. Boom chicka boom.
Boom chicka ricka chicka. Boom, boom, boom.

Appear, appear, appear, we pray,
at the good old Thesmophoree-aye
Oats, peas, beans, and barley grows,
but how they do it, nobody knows.
Boom chicka boom. Boom chicka boom.
Boom chicka ricka chicka. Boom, boom, boom.   1070
(At the end of this performance Euripides returns, thinly disguised as an
old procuress; the chorus recognizes him, the
Scythian does not. He carries a harp, and is
followed by a dancing girl and a young flute-girl.)

EURIPIDES
    Ladies, ladies, ladies. Let's call it a draw. I am willing,
    and I promise never to say anything bad about you, ever again.
    That's my offer. What do you say?

FIRST CHORISTER
    Is it a trick? Why this change of heart?

EURIPIDES
    This poor fish, whom you've got stretched out on a plank,
    is my brother-in-law, I'm sorry to say.
    Give him back to me, and you will have no more cause to
            complain

about anything I write. Otherwise, I shall let all your husbands
      know
what you've been up to while they've been off at the war.

FIRST CHORISTER *(after a moment's consultation with her sisters)*
    We accept the truce, but what about him? There's still the
         Scythian.   1080
(They remain on stage, watching the rest of the action.)

EURIPIDES
    I'll take care of him, don't worry.
(to the dancing girl)
    Come, my little chickadee, do what I told you.
    Go past him and pull up your dress. Let him have a quick flash
    of the old woolly-woolly.
(to the flute-girl)
               And you, you sweet young tart,
    play us the air of a Persian dance.
(Flute-girl commences playing.)

SCYTHIAN SERGEANT *(waking)*
             Das musicalisher opfer? Delizioso!

EURIPIDES
    Auslander, Scythian, Venutian, whatever you are,
    this young thespian is going to practice some dances
    she has to perform at a feast in a couple of hours.

SCYTHIAN SERGEANT
    Okey and dokey by me, kee-mo-sabe; I no get in her way.
    She dance heap good.

EURIPIDES
             Strut your stuff, my dear.   1090
    Shake your little booty right in his face.
    The proof of your dancing is in his pudding.
    Sit down on his knee, why don't you? That's a girl!

SCYTHIAN SERGEANT
  Ah! yes, put your heinie on my knee.
  What a firm little titty! The best in the city!
  Dat's poetry!

EURIPIDES *(to the audience)*
                Dat's pornography. I know it when I see it.
(to the flute-girl)
  More, more! Play that instrument. The Scythian likes it.

SCYTHIAN SERGEANT
  What a tush! What a twat.
  Good und sweet und wet und hot!
  But you keep viggling, I can't get it in . . .   1100

EURIPIDES
  That certainly is true, Ollie!
(to Mnesilochus)
                While he's tearing off a piece,
  it'll be time for us to be tearing off.

SCYTHIAN SERGEANT
                                Give me a kiss.

EURIPIDES
  Kiss him. Let him taste your ware. And your what.

SCYTHIAN SERGEANT
  Oh! oh! oh! Très, très, très jolie. Bella. Bueno. Can we make
                jig-a-jig?

EURIPIDES
  Sorry, no, that's not what I paid her to do.

SCYTHIAN SERGEANT
  Oh! oh! You a mean old bitch. I got to shtup her.

EURIPIDES
    Will you give a drachma?

SCYTHIAN SERGEANT
                    Yah, si, da, oui.

EURIPIDES
    Hand it over.

SCYTHIAN SERGEANT
                    I don't got it on me. You can hold this.
    I pay you later.
(He unstraps his belt with the sword on it and hands it to Euripides.)

EURIPIDES
                    You bring her back here, you hear?

SCYTHIAN SERGEANT *(to the dancing girl)*
    You be coming mit mir.
(giggles; then, to Euripides)
                    And you, lady, you keep an eye on dis fella.   1110
    But what's your name?

EURIPIDES
                    Heidi Fleiss.

SCYTHIAN SERGEANT
                    Howdy, Heidi.
(He takes the dancing girl away.)

EURIPIDES *(aside)*
    It's working out! Just like a goddamn play, isn't it?
(to the flute-girl)
    You go keep them busy, while I untie my friend here.
(to Mnesilochus, whom he begins to untie)
    And you, run along now to my sister and my nephews.

MNESILOCHUS
 I wasn't planning on hanging around.

EURIPIDES *(releasing Mnesilochus)*
 There! It's done. Get out of here.

MNESILOCHUS
 As Herodotus says somewhere, "I'm history!"
(Both depart in haste.)

SCYTHIAN SERGEANT *(returning)*
 What a shtup! My pipes are all ausgecleanen.
 But where is old lady? And the guy!
 Ah shitty shitty shitty! A dirty trick!
 Heidi has fleeced me!
*(He sees the sword belt which has been left behind. He picks it up and
                    throws it across the stage.)*
 Mine own sword and I am cut down.
 The fucking you get ain't worth the fucking you get.
 Heidi! Where the fuck are you?

1120

FIRST CHORISTER
 That nice lady who was here just a moment ago?

SCYTHIAN SERGEANT
 Si. Dove. Where she go?

FIRST CHORISTER *(pointing in the wrong direction)*
                         She left.

SCYTHIAN SERGEANT
                         With the guy?

FIRST CHORISTER
 Right, right. They were together. Running.

SCYTHIAN SERGEANT

    The nasty old bitch! But which way? Left or right? Hey, Heidi!
                Ho there!

FIRST CHORISTER

    No, no, not that way. The other way. You can catch them.
    You'll head them off at the pass.   1130

SCYTHIAN SERGEANT

    I fuck her. They fuck me. I fuck them!
    This one fucking mess, you know that?
(He runs off.)

FIRST CHORISTER *(to the Scythian)*

    Bye-bye. Auf Wiedersehn. Au revoir. Sayonara. Arrivederci.
(and to the audience)

    And to you, too! Ta ta.
    This has dragged on long enough.
    Lezbe-on our way. Time to go home.
    And may the two goddesses bless you and reward us for our
                labors!

Wealth

Translated by
Palmer Bovie

Translator's Preface

Plutus, or *Wealth*, staged in 388 B.C., three years before Aristophanes' death, is the last of his extant plays. It differs in style totally from his earlier dramas, known as Old Comedy, and points forward to the evolving style of New Comedy, perfected by Menander (342–291 B.C.). There are no fantastically imaged choruses of Clouds, Birds, Wasps, and Frogs, offering moral preachments and political advice, no women claiming their right to be heard. Instead, we enter the realistic world of contemporary manners, of common human behavior and misbehavior, and social anxiety. The small chorus provides incidental music punctuating the episodes.

The human characters of *Wealth* are ordinary people in an ordinary predicament, hard pressed to earn a living in democratic Athens. When Apollo places Plutus, a blind, disheveled, unrecognizable figure, in their path, the leading character, Chremylus, and his servant Cario are glad to discover the god's identity and offer him the hospitality of their home. Chremylus has gone to the shrine of Apollo at Delphi, accompanied by Cario, to ask Apollo's advice about bringing up his son. Would it be better to teach him the corrupt tricks and conniving strategies that seem to gain the most success in worldly affairs, or to educate him in virtuous and honest dealing? Apollo vouchsafed no answer but simply instructed Chremylus to follow the first person he met after leaving the shrine, who turned out to be the mysterious blind beggar.

Zeus has made Plutus blind because of his ability to distinguish between good and bad men, rewarding the virtuous. Now he can no longer see which are which. Chremylus devises a plan to take Plutus to the temple of Aesculapius and have the god of Health cure Wealth. As described in a long messenger scene by Cario, the cure is successful and by now, rumors having flown about quickly, everyone is headed toward Chremylus' house. Not the least among them are Chremylus' fellow farmers (forming the chorus), eager to share in the good fortune.

There are, of course, some who object to the fact that wealth is now freely available to all who deserve it, and debates flare up. Poverty, for instance, the goddess of hard luck, argues for the incentive system that drives men to work. With money assured them, she insists, laborers and artisans will no longer produce the necessities and adornments of civilized life. Chremylus and his friend Blepsidemus reply that, with money in hand, they can hire workers from, for example, Thrace or some similarly unenlightened region of Greece. Poverty scolds them furiously and leaves, claiming to have won the argument.

An Honest Man now appears. He had aided his friends when they were hard pressed, but when he needed their help his requests were ignored and he was ruined. Now that Wealth has made him solvent again, he wants to dedicate his ragged cloak and worn shoes to the god as a votive offering. He is warmly welcomed by Chremylus and Cario, but soon accosted by an Informer, who struggles to justify his nefarious conduct by claiming that it only strengthens the case against plaintiffs brought before the actual judges in court. The Informer and his Witness (who follows him everywhere) are driven off the stage under a barrage of scorn from the Honest Man and his partners in virtue, Chremylus and Cario.

An Old Lady complains that Wealth has cost her the attentions of her young lover, no longer in need of her support and favors. She is asked to join the train of Wealth's attendants.

Two gods step forward to find a place in the new dispensation. Hermes, the god of the market and money, laments the lack of the sacrificial offerings he formerly enjoyed, tasty gifts and other forms of compensation. He announces his plan to stay on earth where things are better than in heaven. As for a role, he could advise sales representatives, or help brokers polish their marketing guile. He might fund athletic contests, support for national games and for the arts being the special prerogative of the wealthy. Cario decides that Hermes should be included in the ranks of well-intentioned citizens.

A bizarre candidate rounds off the list, the Priest of Zeus the Savior, now starving and neglected. Formerly, many would offer him generous gifts: a merchant, praying for his ship's safe return; a litigant, grateful for the favorable settling of his case; others, giving thanks by feasting with their many friends and numerous acquaintances. The Priest of Salvation has decided to resign from Zeus' service and live in Athens, where supplies are bountiful. Chremylus offers the unexpected assurance that Zeus is already there, and as the priest is rushing off to find his superior, detains him, appointing him head torch-bearer in the procession to Athena's temple. The entire company (of the deserving) form up for the parade to the Parthenon, where they will install Wealth as the guardian of the Treasury of Athens. Exeunt omnes.

Aristophanes includes gods in his scenario. Apollo sets the action in motion. Plutus is a rather unfamiliar deity. Poverty we have heard of often and has some claim on our attention. The clever financier Hermes sees a way to profit by changing jobs. The supernaturally endowed Aesculapius cures Plutus, but then the Priest of Salvation appears, only to be informed that Zeus is in fact also there. This cannot be literally true, if only because Zeus is never allowed to be presented on the Attic stage. But it can be symbolically true if his influence compensates for the cruel punishment inflicted on a naive God of Wealth. Well-intentioned citizens cannot see that they are being taken advantage of, often victimized. But now this strange new god Plutus is back in a position to see that getting on in life does not mean taking advantage of others.

Cast

PLUTUS, god of wealth
CHREMYLUS, a citizen of Athens
CARIO, Chremylus' servant
CHORUS of farmers, friends of Chremylus
BLEPSIDEMUS, friend of Chremylus
POVERTY, goddess
WIFE of Chremylus
HONEST MAN
INFORMER
OLD LADY
YOUNG MAN
HERMES, god of financial transactions
PRIEST OF ZEUS in charge of Salvation
NONSPEAKING
    Witness

*(The scene, unchanged throughout the play, is a street in Athens
    with the farm house of Chremylus in the background. On stage is
    Wealth, a blind old man, shabbily dressed, groping his way
    forward from the left. He is followed at a middle distance by
    Chremylus, an elderly Athenian citizen, and his slave Cario, who
    brings up the rear. Chremylus and Cario wear bay leaves on
    their heads, indicating that they are returning from a mission to
    consult the oracle of Apollo at Delphi; Cario has in his hand a
    piece of meat from their sacrifice. He grumbles in the opening
    lines.)*

CARIO *(aside)*
    What a pain in the neck it is, O Zeus
    and you other gods above, to be a slave-in-use who's used
    by a crazy master!
    It's a disaster: if you ladle out advice
    as to the best course to follow, he shrinks

from acting on it; so the slave must swallow
the fruits of failure. Fortune thinks
that the natural original owner of the body
is not its owner, the buyer is. THE ONE WHO BOUGHT IT
                    OWNS IT.
But *basta!* Let me file a complaint against Apollo,   10
though, saying the sooth from his golden tripod
up there at Delphi. I'm entitled to it: By god,
he's a physician and a clever diagnostician,
people say, but he sent my owner away in a state
of depression and contradiction; gave him the gate,
instructing him to follow behind the first man he met,
and that man happens to be blind: it's supposed to be
that we who see, lead the blind but how absurd
this looks to be behind without saying a word,
and make me fall in step in this parade.   20
I can't keep quiet about it.

(calls out)

                    HEY, CHIEF!
If you won't tell me why we're following the blind guy,
I'll keep hammering away on the point, keeping
on driving you to distraction. And you can't take action
against me because I enjoy the protection
of this sacred chaplet from Delphi that grants immunity
from beatings.

CHREMYLUS

Lay off your bleatings or, by Zeus, I'll
tear that wreath right off your brow
and make you one big bruise.   30

CARIO

You no make-a sense! I'll keep on asking
who this man is and tasking you with questions
until I'm basking in the knowledge of who it is
we're in tow of. I only want to know for your own
personal good. I'm behind you but I'm on your side.

CHREMYLUS

    Good point: I'll let you in on the secret; after all
    I've found you to be the best slave in my halls,
    as well as the quickest-fingered. So . . . my bio:
    I've been a poor but honest and decent sort,
    not prosperous . . .   40

CARIO

    Not a preposterous statement.

CHREMYLUS

    While temple-robbers, hype-speakers, informers, criminals grew
                rich.

CARIO

    I can trust you on that account.

CHREMYLUS

    So I went to the god to put the question,
    figuring that my own life, an unhappy man's,
    will soon be over, I wondered about my son's:
    would he, my only son, be well advised to change
    his way of life and habits, exchanging them
    for the cheater's way of taking unfair advantage,
    ready for any sort of dirty deal? Such a style   50
    seemed to be the way to success in life.

CARIO

    And what did Phoebus proclaim
    from his sacred wreath domain?

CHREMYLUS

    You'll hear what the god said loud and clear.
    He ordered me to hang on to and not let go of
    the first man I met when I left the sanctuary,
    and to urge that person to come back home with me.

CARIO
> Who was that first man you met?

CHREMYLUS
> This man, already yet.

CARIO
> So then, of course, you got the drift   60
> of the god's prophetic gift, telling you,
> you dumb bunny, in the plainest form of speech,
> to teach your son to practice modern behavior.

CHREMYLUS
> How do you draw that conclusion?

CARIO
> Even a blind man can see the point. The way
> things are at present, it's advantageous
> to not be good, but outrageous.

CHREMYLUS
> That can't have been the oracle's moral;
> if our man here would tell us who he is
> and how and why he came to lead us on his   70
> way, we might divine the oracle's soothsaying.

CARIO *(addressing the blind man)*
> Look! Will you tell us who you are, or shall I
> move to the next item on the agenda?
> *(shaking his fist)*
> Sound off!

WEALTH
> Why don't you go to hell?

CARIO *(to Chremylus)*
> Did you catch that identity?

CHREMYLUS
    It was addressed to you, not me. You didn't phrase
    the question properly.

CHREMYLUS *(approaching the blind man)*
    If you have any respect
    for and are pleased to find an honest man,   80
    tell me who you are.

WEALTH
    What I say is: damn you!

CARIO *(to Chremylus)*
    Take over. The oracle's in your court.

CHREMYLUS *(shaking his head at the blind man)*
    Demeter'll beat your bones
    for what you just said.

CARIO *(to Wealth)*
    If you don't speak up I'll lay you flat and that'll
    be that.

WEALTH
    See here, my friends, please leave me alone.

CHREMYLUS
    But of course!

CARIO
    Chief, take my advice: it's the best. I'll knock   90
    him off, guide him up to a cliffside rock,
    and leave him standing there while i take off.
    But he steps forward, and makes off in the wrong
    neck-breaking direction to sever his connection
    with life.

CHREMYLUS
    Let's get on with it, then: take him away.
(Both grab the blind man.)

WEALTH
    Oh, no! No!

CHREMYLUS
    So, why not speak?

WEALTH
    If you're told who I am, I am in no doubt
    you'll do me some damage and won't let me go . . .   100

CHREMYLUS
    Oh, we'll let you off, if that's what you want,

WEALTH
    First, let go of me.

CHREMYLUS
    There you go.
(They release him.)

WEALTH
    Listen carefully: I suppose I must spill a secret
    I was planning to keep. I'm Plutus, the God of Wealth.

CHREMYLUS
    Oh, what a rogue and peasant slave you are!
    The worst. To be Wealth all this time and keep it
    in the dark!

CARIO
    Wealth? In rags?

CHREMYLUS
> Phoebus Apollo! O ye Gods! O ye demigods!   110
> Zeus, what news! What's that you're saying?
> You are in fact Wealth?

WEALTH
> In fact, and curiously enough, intact.

CHREMYLUS
> The very one?

WEALTH
> Himself.

CHREMYLUS
> Where have you been just now in such a downtrodden state?

WEALTH
> I've just been at Patrocles' house. You know,
> he's never washed himself since the day he was born.

CHREMYLUS
> And what brought about that malodorous mistake?

WEALTH
> Zeus did that to me, out of jealousy   120
> toward the human race. When I was a boy
> I crowed about how I would only visit men
> who were honest, wise, and virtuous: and thus
> he blinded me so I could not recognize any such.
> Good men make him jealous.

CHREMYLUS
> But it's the good, trustworthy ones who are zealous
> in honoring him.

WEALTH
    Point well taken.

CHREMYLUS
    Now think: if you regained your former sight
    would you still withhold your favor from the blight   130
    of scoundrels?

WEALTH
    With all my might.

CHREMYLUS
    And just go to the just?

WEALTH
    With gusto! I haven't laid eyes on them
    for a long time now.

CHREMYLUS *(peering into the audience)*
    As far as I can see, me neither.

WEALTH
    You can let me go now. I've told you my story.

CHREMYLUS
    No. Listen please: hear my plea,
    and don't abandon me. If you keep on
    looking for an honest man, you'll never   140
    light on one more respectable than me.

CARIO
    Not one, except for me.

WEALTH
    So I see: that's what they all always say.
    But when they've really gotten hold of me
    and prosper, they start in all over again
    on their shenanigans.

CHREMYLUS
>Very true. But not everybody is bad.

WEALTH
>Not true. Every single son of a mother
>is another example of one bad apple.

CARIO *(to himself)*
>I bet you're gonna regret you said that.   150

CHREMYLUS
>Now lend me your ear, so you can learn and hear
>the advantages coming your way if you'll only stay
>with *us*. *Plus*: I think, I really do figure—
>and I say this knowing that God may be listening—
>that, so help us God, I'll be able to set you free
>from this blindness and make you see.

WEALTH
>Back off! I'm not the least interested
>in seeing again.

CHREMYLUS
>What's that you say?

CARIO
>The fellow was born to be miserable.   160

WEALTH
>Zeus will grind me into dust if he only just
>gets word of how depraved these mortals are.

CHREMYLUS
>But isn't he grinding you down right now
>by sending you stumbling along?

WEALTH

>Maybe so, but you know I'm terribly afraid
>of the heavenly fellow.

CHREMYLUS

>Can it be so? You, a heaven-dweller yourself,
>a low-down coward deity shrinking with velleity?
>You think that Zeus, for all his sovereignty
>and thunderbolts would add up at all to an obol   170
>if you could see again, if only briefly?

WEALTH

>You con man, don't say things like that!

CHREMYLUS

>Hold your tongue and let me prove to you
>that you have much more power at your disposal
>than Zeus can use.

WEALTH

>You'll prove I'm stronger?

CHREMYLUS

>That I'll do. For instance, let me ask my man, Cario:
>by what means does Zeus exercise his rule
>over the gods?

CARIO

>By money, good, hard cash, no credit cards. Besides,   180
>he's cornered the money market.

CHREMYLUS

>And who keeps his coffers crammed with cash?

CARIO

>Our man here.

CHREMYLUS

And when men sacrifice, isn't this what they pray for?

CARIO

No doubt about it. No one pretends he doesn't pray
to be rich.

CHREMYLUS

So, that makes him the prime mover. And he
could easily put an end to all this if he
had a mind to.

WEALTH

Oh, yes? Just how?   190

CHREMYLUS

Because if you refused your consent not a man
would make one sacrifice, no, not of an ox
or a barley-cake or anything else at all.

WEALTH

And why would this be so?

CHREMYLUS

Be so? Because they couldn't buy a thing
unless you're right there handing out the cash.
If Zeus abuses you in any way, it's you alone
who can bring him down.

WEALTH

You're saying they sacrifice to him by means of me?

CHREMYLUS

Just what I'm saying. All that is magnificent to man,   200
and beautiful, and charming, this all comes about
through you. Everything bows down to wealth.

CARIO

>Take me, for example. A smidgen of ready cash
>made me a slave. I couldn't match their money.

CHREMYLUS

>The ladies of easy virtue languishing in Corinth
>say that when a poor man asks for their favors
>they pay him no never mind, but when a rich character
>sidles up to them they'll stoop to anything.

CARIO

>And wanton boys, I'm told, are just the same—
>they'll do anything for money, but not for love.   210

CHREMYLUS

>The kept boys, you mean: the "Ganymedes," but not
>good boys. They don't ask you for money.

CARIO

>What do they ask for?

CHREMYLUS

>A good-looking horse, perhaps, or a pack of hounds.

CARIO

>Well, they could be too embarrassed to ask for money,
>so they coat over their misconduct by concocting
>another name for it.

CHREMYLUS

>All men's arts and techniques have been discovered
>through you. One man sticks to his last and cobbles
>shoes; another works hard at the forge as a smith;   220
>another is a carpenter; another is a goldsmith, gilding
>with the gold he gets from you. And, by Zeus, another
>steals clothes off the rack; another's a one-story man
>or washes clothes . . .

CARIO
Cleans sheepskins, dresses hides, sells onions.

CHREMYLUS
By your means the sex abuser, the guilty seducer,
gets off with a light sentence.

WEALTH
Well, whoa! Woe is me! To think I didn't know
all this earlier along!

CARIO
Doesn't the king of Persia puff up with pride   230
on his peacock throne because of his wealth?
And the representatives in the house of the Assembly
clutch the power of the purse by buying their way in?
And don't you man the triremes?

CHREMYLUS
Don't you feed and supply the mercenary troops
besieging Corinth?

CARIO
How about Pamphilus the embezzler? Wasn't he caught
by means of you? And his side-kick "the Needle Man"?
Agyrrhius, who's so well fed, blows it out his fat
ass, thanks to you?
(turning to Wealth)
                                    Philepsius   240
spins out his slanders with your help. Our alliance
with the Egyptians in their plan to subvert the Persians
was backed by you. And Lais—or was her name Nais?—
in her love for that dissolute rotten rich Philonides,
was led into it by you. Then there's the tower
pompous Timotheus trumped up in the middle of town . . .

CHREMYLUS *(to Cario)*
    I wish it would fall on you.
(to Wealth)
    Whatever we do is transacted through you.
    You're at the root of it all, our misfortunes as well
    as our good fortunes, let me assure you.   250

CARIO
    In war, for sure, the side wealth backs
    never loses.

WEALTH
    Can I, one single force, effect so many results?

CHREMYLUS
    Yes, by Zeus, and a lot more things than these . . .
    The result is that no one has ever been satiated
    with you. There's plenty enough of other things:
    Of love . . .

CARIO
    Of bread . . .

CHREMYLUS
    Of art . . .

CARIO
    Of candy . . .   260

CHREMYLUS
    Of honor . . .

CARIO
    Of cake . . .

CHREMYLUS
    Of manly courage . . .

CARIO
Of figs . . .

CHREMYLUS
Of ambition . . .

CARIO
Of barley buns . . .

CHREMYLUS
Of military command . . .

CARIO
Of lentil soup . . .

CHREMYLUS
But no one ever has it up to here with you.
Someone gets thirteen thousand: he's all the more   270
interested in amassing sixteen. When he has that,
he'll have to have forty, or life, he laments, is not
worth living . . .

WEALTH
What an eloquent speech! But there's still one thing
I'm afraid of.

CHREMYLUS
And what may that be?

WEALTH
This power you say I have. I don't see how
I can get control of it.

CHREMYLUS
Just like you. Of course, everybody keeps saying
that wealth is the most fearful scaredy-cat.   280

WEALTH

That's not the way it goes. A burglar started the rumor
when be broke into my house one day and found
everything under lock and key and couldn't lay hands
on a single item; he said my painstaking prudence
was a form of cowardice.

CHREMYLUS

Let not your heart be troubled. If you're keen
for the job, I'll make your eyesight even keener
than Lynceus', the lookout on the Argo.

WEALTH

But look: you're only mortal, so how can you
manage that?   290

CHREMYLUS

I'll follow the feeling I got when Apollo
brandished the bay leaves my way, and spoke up.

WEALTH

He was in on the secret?

CHREMYLUS

Oh yes, indeed.

WEALTH

Better watch your step!

CHREMYLUS

Don't worry your head over that, my friend.
Rest assured: I'll carry it through to the end,
even if it ends my life.

CARIO

Me too, if you'll agree.

CHREMYLUS

    And lots of others will side with us, good men   300
    who've gone without bread.

WEALTH

    A shabby sort of reinforcements!

CHREMYLUS

    Not at all, once they're rich as they used to be.
(to Cario)
    Now dash off, you . . .

CARIO

    Me, move? Where to?

CHREMYLUS

    To call my fellow farmers in from the fields
    out there, working away. Say that I want each man
    to come in and share this piece of Plutus with us.

CARIO

    I'm off and running. But have someone from inside
    the house take care of this meat, my sacrifice take-out.   310

CHREMYLUS *(takes the meat)*

    I'll take care of that, right away
(Exit Cario.)
    Now, Wealth, most powerful one, do just step inside
    my house. Here it is, right here: this is the house
    you must fill, by fair means or foul, with wealth today.

WEALTH

    I'm worried, though, really worried about having to go
    into other people's houses; I never ever had any profit
    from it. If I happened to enter a miser's miserable
    quarters, he would dig a deep hole and bury me in it

right away; then, if some good type came by and asked
for a bit of cash to tide him over, he'd roundly declare   320
that he'd never laid eyes on me. And if I happened to enter
a profligate spendthrift's domain, I'd be poured out
for a bimbo's favors, and in no time all be driven out
stripped to the buff.

CHREMYLUS

Yup: that's rough. It's because you never met up with
a moderate man: a character like me, consistent.
I delight in saving, as much as any other man, *plus*
I don't mind shelling out, when needed. Let's go in;
I want my wife to meet you, and my son, the one I dote on
most of all, after you.   330

WEALTH

Right. After you.

CHREMYLUS

Why would anyone shrink from telling the truth to you?
(They exit. It's time for an interlude of music. The Chorus of Athenian
                   farmers comes tumbling in, behind Cario.)

CARIO

Ah, time-sharers! Many a time
you've eaten the same thyme with my master, good friends
and neighbors, and hardworking labor-lovers; come along.
Get a move on, this is no time to stall, not at all.
It's a critical moment and you should be in on it
and help us out.

CHORUS LEADER

Can't you see how we're hustling down the track
like an ant with lumbago, as reasonably as can   340
be hoped for from a weak old man? You seem to think
I ought to break into a run before you've even told me

the purpose of this exercise, and why your master orders me
to come on it.

CARIO

I've *been* telling you; you haven't been listening.
The chief says you all will be rid of your cold-hearted,
miserable life and live happily ever after.

LEADER

How on earth can this ever come to pass?

CARIO

Good friends, he's brought back here this old geezer,
an old fogey draped in dirt, halfway bent over, riddled   350
with wretched wrinkles, no hair on his head, no teeth.
And I wouldn't be surprised if he was circumcised.

LEADER

O marvelous messenger, what's with your golden words?
You're letting on that he's come here with a pile of money.

CARIO

What he's got is a sackful of advanced geriatric ills.

LEADER

Geriatric, pediatric, cut the kidding: you don't think
you'll get off without a flick as long as I've got my stick.

CARIO

You consider me someone of naturally bad character?
You think I could say something that is simply not true?

LEADER

Oh what a rogue and pompous peasant slave you are!   360
Your legs are crying out loud, shrieking for their beating,
frantic to place their investments in stocks and bonds.

CARIO

But you've drawn your letter, the letter S, for Sepulcher.
You'll be circuit court judges in the carousel of Hell;
and Charon gives free tickets. So why hang around?

LEADER

Oh, the hell and gone with you, some cheek, you son of a creep,
born for scorn. But you can't fool us; even now you've had
no time to tell us the reason why your master has summoned
me here, or any of us who have hurried hither pronto,
although we really didn't have the time and were worn out   370
with work, and still had a lot of tasty thyme to uproot.
We still got here fast.

CARIO

All right, then. I won't keep it from you any longer.
Gentlemen: my master is here with Plutus, or, Wealth,
and he will make you all rich.

LEADER

Is that a possibility, that we can all be rich?

CARIO

Millionaire Midases! You'll only need asses' ears!

LEADER

If what you say is true, I'll bubble over with pleasure.
And, so lifted up, I'd like to dance for joy.

CARIO

Well, then: let me lead you on in a song and dance,   380
a performance of "The Cyclops." Threttanelo! Look
at this monster rising up, and *en point* on his feet
as well. Isn't that swell? Now you guys get goating
along in lecherous rhythm, bleating like sheep after me

and, like sperm-spraying goats, sounding off on your war
to a succulent mouthful of slurped up breakfast food . . .

LEADER

And we, of *coarse*, will search out the Cyclops, who's bleating
like the chairman at a meeting, and when we find you
in your chaotic office quarters, with your leather briefcase
bursting at the seams with fresh-cut greens, debauched,   390
flat out on your couch, head shepherd of some mini-sheep
sleeping somewhere or other—then we'll get hold of
a big burning stake and try our best to blind you.

CARIO

But then I'll don my Circe persona. She's a oner
at mixing and stirring drugs. Just a while ago, you remember,
she tricked the friends of Philonides—you remember
Philonides, Mister Rotten Rich?—into thinking that they
were boars, and got them to dine on dung, a pasta
she cleverly kneaded into burgers for them?
And you'll get the same medication. So follow me, kids   400
and skivvies, pig along and out after mother.

LEADER

Ah, so! You're playing Circe's role now, are you?
Her part is concocting and mixing drugs, hell bent
on defiling and fouling up our companions, that's it?
Well . . . like the son of Laertes, who took delicious delight
in hanging you up by the balls and plastering your nostril
with dung like a billy-goat's. And you, gasping for air,
will say, "Follow your mother sow anyhow, you swine."

CARIO

Ok. The joke's over. That's enough heavy comedy.
Change back into your original shapes. I've got to go   410
now, before my master gets back, and take on some bread
and meat. EAT. Then we've got work to do.
(*Chremylus enters.*)

CHREMYLUS

    Welcome, neighbors! But that's a dated form
    of greeting, so I'll say "How are you?" and give you a hug
    for coming so promptly and energetically and not dragging your
        feet.

LEADER

    Don't worry about it; we're on the warpath.
    It would be silly if we, jostled around willy-nilly
    in the Assembly to pick up our pay of three obols a day,
    were to hand over Plutus to someone to take away.

CHREMYLUS

    Ah now, I see Blepsidemus showing up, bustling   420
    along like an ant just cured of lumbago. In view
    of the speed he's making he's heard about our undertaking.
(Blepsidemus enters.)

BLEPSIDEMUS *(to himself)*

    What's this business? How can Chremylus
    come up so rich all of a sudden, and where's it from?
    I just don't believe it, and yet I swear there was talk
    among the customers lounging around the barber shops
    about how be had suddenly struck it rich. But what
    has me guessing is the fact that he's summoned his friends
    to share the wealth. That's not normal procedure here.

CHREMYLUS *(aside)*

    Well, I'll spill it out then, and not keep anything   430
    back.
(to Blepsidemus)
        Blepsidemus, my lad, we're
    much better off than we were yesterday,
    so you are quite welcome to share; we are friends.

BLEPSIDEMUS

    Is it true what they say, you're a wealthy man?

CHREMYLUS

    Not exactly. But if it's God's wish I'll be rich soon.
    At the moment there's a bit of risk involved.

BLEPSIDEMUS

    Risk, tsk! What kind of risk?
    The kind . . .
    Hurry up. Out with it.

CHREMYLUS

    If we pull off what we're trying to pull off,   440
    we'll always prosper. But if we fail we are sure
    to be ruined.

BLEPSIDEMUS

    I don't like the looks of that. Your freight-load
    frightens me. All at once you're richer than rich;
    and yet you're anxious about it. That role is played
    by someone who's pulled off a shady deal.

CHREMYLUS

    What's so shady about it?

BLEPSIDEMUS

    What I mean is: if you've come back from the shrine
    with some gold or silver lifted from the god, are
    now sorry for your action, or transaction . . .   450

CHREMYLUS

    Oh, no, God forbid! Apollo would never swallow that.

BLEPSIDEMUS

    Stop hollerin' foolishness. My good friend:
    it's all quite obvious.

CHREMYLUS

    How can you think such a thing of me?

BLEPSIDEMUS

I'll tell you how. There's not a scrap of good
sound goodness left in anyone these days. Everyone
is a slave to the ceaseless desire for gain.

CHREMYLUS

By Ceres, your cerebration suffers from dislocation.

BLEPSIDEMUS *(aside)*

How the man has changed from what he was!

CHREMYLUS

You're moping, you dope.   460

BLEPSIDEMUS *(aside)*

So shifty-eyed, the criminal's crooked look.

CHREMYLUS

I know what you're glunking about like a frog.
You think I stole something and (glunk!)
you want your share.

BLEPSIDEMUS

I want a share? A share of what?

CHREMYLUS

Fact is, it's not the way you think it is, quite different.

BLEPSIDEMUS

Robbery and assault, not just larceny?

CHREMYLUS

You must be possessed. You're obsessed.

BLEPSIDEMUS

What you mean to say is: you haven't embezzled
someone's money?   470

CHREMYLUS
>   Not a cent. I hav*en't*.

BLEPSIDEMUS
>   By Heracles, where on earth can I turn? You're not at
>   all inclined to tell me the truth.

CHREMYLUS
>   But you're charging me with crime before the fact.

BLEPSIDEMUS
>   My friend, I'll make it my job to settle this
>   with only minor costs. I'll turn off the blabbermouths,
>   by shutting them up with some small change.

CHREMYLUS
>   Probably laying out three bucks for your efforts,
>   and sending me a twelve-dollar bill for your services.

BLEPSIDEMUS
>   I can envisage an old man sitting in a court,   480
>   holding out a suppliant's olive bough, surrounded by
>   his wife and children: a scene to match the portrait
>   of *The Children of Heracles* in Pamphilus' famous painting.

CHREMYLUS
>   No, you lunkhead. I'll make things work out so that
>   from now only the good citizens, the intelligent ones,
>   the self-effacing are able to be men of wealth.

BLEPSIDEMUS
>   What's that? You've stolen all that much?

CHREMYLUS
>   Troubles, troubles! I'll be doubled over with your barbs.

BLEPSIDEMUS
   No, you can fold up yourself all by yourself, seems to me.

CHREMYLUS
   No, I won't. And you know why? Because I've got Wealth,   490
   you miserable mutt.

BLEPSIDEMUS
   Wealth? Plutus? What Plutus?

CHREMYLUS
   The god himself.

BLEPSIDEMUS
   Where?

CHREMYLUS
   Inside.

BLEPSIDEMUS
   Inside where?

CHREMYLUS
   My place.

BLEPSIDEMUS
   Your house?

CHREMYLUS
   That's the place.

BLEPSIDEMUS
   I'll be damned! Plutus is in your house?   500

CHREMYLUS
   I swear.

BLEPSIDEMUS
You're saying the truth?

CHREMYLUS
I am.

BLEPSIDEMUS
By Hestia—

CHREMYLUS
and by good old Poseidon.

BLEPSIDEMUS
The god of the sea?

CHREMYLUS
If there's another sea god, count him in.

BLEPSIDEMUS
But you're not sending him around to your friends,
all of us?

CHREMYLUS
Well, the situation hasn't quite reached that point.   510

BLEPSIDEMUS
What point? The sharing point or the point share?

CHREMYLUS
By Zeus, not yet. First of all we have to . . .

BLEPSIDEMUS
Do what?

CHREMYLUS
Make him see again.

BLEPSIDEMUS
  Who he?

CHREMYLUS
  Wealth, of course. As he used to see before.

BLEPSIDEMUS
  Really blind, is he?

CHREMYLUS
  By the heavens, yes!

BLEPSIDEMUS
  No wonder he never came by to see me.

CHREMYLUS
  But if the gods are willing, he'll be calling now.   520

BLEPSIDEMUS
  Shouldn't we be calling the doctor?

CHREMYLUS
  What doctor is there in the city? The profession
  is out of practice when there aren't any fees to earn.

BLEPSIDEMUS
  Let's think it through.

CHREMYLUS
  There's not a single one.

BLEPSIDEMUS
  You're right.

CHREMYLUS
  By Zeus, we'll use the ruse I've planned on
  for some time now. We'll lay him out on a couch
  in the temple of Aesculapius.

BLEPSIDEMUS

    Excellent plan! Let's not lag: let's get on   530
    with something or other.

CHREMYLUS

    I'm off, then.

BLEPSIDEMUS

    Then hurry up.

CHREMYLUS

    I'm up and running.
    (He hurries off, Blepsidemus in tow. They are met by a hideous hag who
                confronts them with a rasping voice.)

POVERTY

    You weirdos! How dare you take such precipitous
    steps? Wicked, illegal! So you're off, are you,
    to . . . just where?

BLEPSIDEMUS

    Heracles! Help!

POVERTY

    I'll wreck you wretches in the most wreckest way
    to be wrecked. Things neither god nor man   540
    has had to endure before. You're done for.

CHREMYLUS

    Who are you? You don't look at all well. So pale.

BLEPSIDEMUS

    Maybe she's a Fury, fresh from some tragedy:
    she's got that long-drawn, melancholy look.

CHREMYLUS

    No Fury. She hasn't got a torch.

BLEPSIDEMUS
>We'll punch out her lights for that.

POVERTY
>Just who do you think I am?

CHREMYLUS
>Bartender, barmaid, or a pancake flipper.
>Otherwise, you wouldn't have opened up on us
>like that.   550

POVERTY
>Aren't you ashamed of yourselves for trying
>to lock me out everywhere and banish me?

CHREMYLUS
>Well, there's always the Bottom Line. You could
>just drop down dead. Now: who are you, exactly?

POVERTY
>I'm who today will demand satisfaction from you
>for trying to exile me from everywhere.

BLEPSIDEMUS
>Isn't that the barmaid from the local, the one
>who always waters the drinks?

POVERTY
>I've been living with you two now, for years.
>My name is POVERTY.   560

BLEPSIDEMUS
>King Apollo, Zeus, and the others, zut, alors!
>*(starts to move)*
>Where can a guy go now?

CHREMYLUS
  Hey, you! What's up, you scaredy-cat? Stop!

BLEPSIDEMUS
  Stopping's the last item on my shopping list

CHREMYLUS
  Hang on. Can one woman scare off two men?

BLEPSIDEMUS
  Yes, you wrack and ruin; she's POVERTY,
  and there's no living being anywhere on earth
  who's more ruinous.
(He starts off again.)

CHREMYLUS
  Hold it, I beg you.

BLEPSIDEMUS
  The answer is NO.   570

CHREMYLUS
  It'd be a crying shame to run away now
  and leave our good god unprotected, not
  fight it out, just because we're afraid of her.

BLEPSIDEMUS
  Leaning on what force or trusty weapons?
  Some measly spear-proof jacket, or a shield
  this excuse for a woman hasn't put in pawn?

CHREMYLUS
  This god of ours alone will be surety to
  triumph over the old bag's bag of tricks.

POVERTY

> You've got the nerve to mumble, over there,
> when you miserable mutts have been caught in the act   580
> of a horrid crime after the fact?

CHREMYLUS

> And you, old fool of a cesspool, why do you
> tool out here and bash us with a tongue-lashing,
> when we haven't done you any harm?

POVERTY

> No harm? By the gods above, you think you're not
> hurting me when you try to make Wealth see again?

CHREMYLUS

> Say again. If we cudgel our brains doing good
> for all men, how can we be wronging you?

POVERTY

> And what benefit could you come up with?

CHREMYLUS

> Benefit? For starters, we scare you right out of Greece.   590

POVERTY

> Run me off? What worse wrong can you come up with
> than that for men?

CHREMYLUS

> What worse wrong? If we forgot to do what we intend to.

POVERTY

> All right: let's debate that point right now.
> If I can prove that I'm the one and only cause
> that comes your way, that your very lives depend
> on me, then it's fine. But if the point that's mine
> isn't taken, then go ahead and do what you think is best.

CHREMYLUS

    How can you say such a thing, you sad sack of dirt?

POVERTY

    Give it a listen. It's perfectly simple. I'll prove   600
    you're wrong to contend that honest men
    should become the wealthy ones.

BLEPSIDEMUS

    Holy smoke! What we need here is the stocks and bonds.

POVERTY

    Don't yammer with that clamor before you've heard
    what case I'm pleading.

BLEPSIDEMUS

    But who wouldn't shout right out, to hear
    the stuff you're dishing out?

POVERTY

    Anyone in his senses.

CHREMYLUS

    What damages can I claim if you lose the suit?

POVERTY

    Whatever amount you want.   610

CHREMYLUS

    Good! I'll do that.

POVERTY

    When you fix the price it will also entice
    the same amount from you if you lose.

BLEPSIDEMUS

    Will twenty deaths be enough?

CHREMYLUS
  For her, yes. But for us two will do.

POVERTY
  You can't be too quick about it. Is there
  a single valid argument to bring up against me?
  (Chorus enters for a short musical interlude.)

CHORUS LEADER
  To conquer this woman in argument, you'll have
  to have a very clever line. You can't femininely
  back off, you can't yield an inch.   620

CHREMYLUS
  Here's the pitch: it goes without saying,
  much less debating, that it would only be just
  for good men to prosper, while the rascals
  and ungodfearing rogues meet the opposite fate.
  Because we wanted to have this happen, we've gone
  to the trouble to design a plan that's excellent,
  sensitive, and all-around useful. If Wealth sees
  once more and does not go around blind, he may
  make his way straightaway to the precincts of those
  among us who are good and not leave them in the lurch.   630
  He'll want to make his getaway from the evil and from
  the nongodfearing. And so, I imagine he'll manage
  to make all mankind honest and virtuous.
  Can there be some fellow with a proposition better
  to propose?

BLEPSIDEMUS
  Not a one. I'll bear witness to that. No need
  to call on her.

CHREMYLUS
  As things stand today, they're all crazy, or
  stark raving mad: men are possessed. Can you draw

any other conclusion? Many who are the worst   640
and the wealthiest have piled up their riches
by getting around the law, but many good men
are badly off: they're hungry; they hang out

(to Poverty)

with you. There's a better way
of life, I say for people to benefit from
if Plutus got his eyesight back and put the sack
to *her*.

POVERTY

Oh, you two nutty old goofballs, so easily suckered,
partners of the high-stepping throngs of ghouls
and drooling fools, if it happened to you   650
the way you want it to, it wouldn't benefit you.
If Plutus regained the use of his eyes, and dished
out the loot equally, no one would work, not the
artists, not the scientists. With these gone,
thanks to your kind intervention, who'd be willing
to be a blacksmith or ship-builder, or to sew?
Be a wheelwright, a brickmaker? To wash, clean wool,
tan hides, break up the soil of the earth with
ploughs, harvest Demeter's fruits—if you
could all live at ease and neglect all these tasks?   660

CHREMYLUS

Ridiculous! Our servants will ply all these trades.
Every one you've just mentioned.

POVERTY

Servants? What servants? From where?

CHREMYLUS

From the market, paid for in cash.

POVERTY

So, give us the name of the eager seller.

CHREMYLUS

There'll be some greedy guy out there itching
to sell; a merchant just in from Thessaly
where there's a center for hardened perpetrators
to be bought out.

POVERTY

See here: if we follow your course, in due course   670
There won't by any groups to be rounded up. Who
among the healthy will want to round up the dangerous
dogies, at the risk of his own life? Logic
shows that you'll have to wield the plough, and do
the digging, and do the other hard work yourself.
You'll have to live a much harder life than at present.

CHREMYLUS

Let it crash on your head!

POVERTY

What's more, you won't be able to sleep in a bed—
there won't be a bed—or on a nice carpet. Who
will be willing to weave carpets when he has gold?   680
When you lead your bride home you won't present her
with oils and perfumes, or deck her out
in fashionable sheaths richly dyed in different colors . . .
So what good does it do you to be rich
when you can't get these things? From me,
on the other hand, this stuff is easy to come by.
I sit and confront the skilled workers
with their poverty and their need of a source of income.

CHREMYLUS

What can you pick up except a bunch of blisters
when the needy get too close to the stove at the baths   690
to ward off the winter cold? Or a set of hungry children
and plenty of gnats, lice, and fleas that buzz me
to get up and get going, swarming around my head,

to bug me and wake me up, sounding off:
"You'll go hungry! get going!" And the blessings
you have to offer to all: a rag, not a cloak;
a straw mattress teeming with creepy creatures
that arouse sleepy creatures; a mat full of holes,
instead of a rug; for your bed a good-sized stone,
not a pillow; mallow shoots to chew on, and fake bread;   700
withered radish roots instead of barley bread;
for a seat, the rim of a broken jar; a kneading trough?
No: use the sides of a broken one, instead. This list
(hisses sibilantly)
  consists of the items
  on your agenda, doesn't it?

POVERTY
  What you've given is not my bio, oh my, no!
  You've sounded out the beggar's life on your lute.

CHREMYLUS
  Beggary's Poverty's sister, they say. I can see
  why they link them together.

POVERTY
  I imagine you would link up Tyrant and National Hero;   710
  Dionysius would be a Thrasybulus. But my way of life
  isn't set up that way. Zeus would never allow it.
  The beggar's life you describe is nothing, it's full
  of emptiness. A poor man is frugal; he pays attention
  to his work. He doesn't have anything left over, yet
  you're talking nonsense and flapping your wings.

CHREMYLUS
  But why does everyone give you the cold shoulder?

POVERTY
  Because I improve them. You see that at its best
  in children. They flinch away from their fathers,

who are well disposed toward them. It's intricate   720
to pick out the right thing to do.

CHREMYLUS

And you're saying that Zeus can't make the distinction
between what to do and what not? He has wealth.

BLEPSIDEMUS

And sends it down to us.

POVERTY

Oh, you're both mind-boggled, saddled
with out-of-date ideas. Zeus is a pauper. Let me
make my point clear. If he were rich, when presiding
at the Olympic Games every fifth year with the assembled
Greeks, would he crown the victors with olive wreaths
after announcing them? If he has the wherewithal,   730
shouldn't he be crowning them with gold?

CHREMYLUS

This is precisely the way he shows how thrifty he is,
and pays honor to riches at the same time. He does not
want to spend his money, and so he crowns the victors
with baubles and keeps his wealth at his side.

POVERTY

You pin a more disgraceful label on him when you call
him stingy and greedy rather than plain poor.

CHREMYLUS

Of course, Zeus may drive you into the ground
crowning you with a chaplet woven of wild olive.

POVERTY

How dare you contradict me and deny that your blessings   740
derive from Poverty?

CHREMYLUS

    Hear this from Hecate, whether 'tis better
    to be well off or to be hungry.
    She'll surely tell you that the rich folks,
    herr schafften, send meals every once a month
    to be set at her shrine; and then the poor folks
    snatch away this honey before it gets to the hive.
    So much for you! Now just lay off the complaining.
    Put a clamp on it! You'll never persuade me,
    no matter how hard you try.   750

POVERTY

    As Euripides said, "Oh, my city of Argos!"

CHREMYLUS

    Call in Pauson the painter, your dinner companion.

POVERTY

    WOE IS ME!

CHREMYLUS

    WHOA! GO TO HELL AND GONE!

POVERTY

    Where *is* that, exactly?

CHREMYLUS

    How should I know? Just go! And not so damn slow.

POVERTY

    I'll let you off with a warning: the day will come
    when you'll want me back.

CHREMYLUS

    Well, welcome back, *then*. Meanwhile, I'm much
    better off, you mutt, being well off. Rant   760

and rave all you want: "Convince a man against his will:
he's of the same opinion still."
(Exit Poverty.)

BLEPSIDEMUS

By Zeus, I'm on your side. I'd like to be rich,
and have plenty of good stuff to bestow on the wife
and children when I come home sleek and shining
from the baths and can fart in the face of the artisans
and of poverty.

CHREMYLUS

There goes that old bitch. Now you and I
must find a bed for the god in Aesculapius' shrine.

BLEPSIDEMUS

Agreed. No more delay, or someone else will drop by   770
and stall our project.

CHREMYLUS

Cario, boy! Bring that bedding out here
and head up the detail to Aesculapius' quarters
in high-stepping fashion. Have all arrangements made.
(Exeunt omnes. Chorus enters for a musical interlude. A night passes,
and in the morning Cario enters, bearing good
news. He addresses the Chorus.)

CARIO

Ah, old men, who have so often sopped up soup,
with very little bread, at the Feast of Theseus,
learn how you prosper and are in the best of circumstances,
as are all others who lead the untrammeled life of virtue.

LEADER   ·

How now, oh best of all your fellow slaves?
You seem to be bearing good news.   780

CARIO

My master's plan has worked out perfectly.
Or perhaps I should say: Wealth has prospered.
Instead of being blind, this Plutus has had his sight
restored. Aesculapius is a patient-friendly doctor,
and Wealth is now all clear in his pupils.

LEADERS *(leads the Chorus in a line from the Greek National Anthem)*
"Oh joy, oh rapture!"

CARIO

Yes, whether we want to or not, let's capture
the moment of bliss.

LEADER *(another line from the anthem)*
"Let's all
clap our hands for Aesculapius, and for spring,   790
singing of the light he has left us."
(Chremylus' wife, hearing the voices in song, comes out of the house.)

WIFE

Why all these joyful shouts? Has good news come out,
after all? I've just been dreaming about it, sitting down
beside the hourglass, waiting for himself to come.

CARIO

Oh mistress, quickly—bring us some wine
and have some yourself—
(aside)
                                    (you don't mind
a nip now and then). I'm bringing you a mess
of good tidings.
(Wine jar and cups are brought out from the house.)

WIFE

Well, where are they, my husband and the others?

CARIO *(taking a sip of wine)*
    Just a moment and I'll tell . . .   800

WIFE
    Let's get on with the story.

CARIO
    Listen up and I'll have the whole kit and caboodle,
    from the toe right up to the noodle.

WIFE
    Don't footzle around with my noodle.

CARIO
    You want me to just skim off the top.

WIFE
    No, I want the whole crop that's just come in.

CARIO
    When we arrived at the holy shrine, with a man
    who was most wretched then but now is swimming
    in happiness and good luck, we first escorted him
    down to the sea for a bath.   810

WIFE
    Some stroke of luck for an old guy
    to bathe in the icy ocean!

CARIO
    We proceeded to the temple grounds, where our seed-cakes
    and other sacrificial gear were blessed and offered
    as "fuel to the fire god's furnace," so to speak.
    This preceded our stretching out Plutus on a couch,
    while each of us made up our bed of straw.

WIFE

Had any others come for help?

CARIO

Yes: there was Neocleides, the blind man;
he can outsteal many who see perfectly well.   820
Other patients came, in droves, with a list
of many kinds of diseases. At this point the sacristan
put out the lamps and told us to go to sleep.
If we heard a noise we were to stay silent.
So we all lay down and didn't stir up any trouble . . .
Not me: I couldn't drop off, I was all worked up
by a pot of stew beside an old woman's head
that I had a terrible urge to crawl over toward.
So then, when I looked up I saw the priest
snatching up the dried figs and cakes from the altar.   830
He looked all around at the smaller tables
to see if any of the cakes had been left behind
and blessed them by stuffing them in a sack.
I figured this for prescribed pious ritual,
so I got up and headed for that pot of stew.

WIFE

How rash! Weren't you afraid of the god?

CARIO

Sure enough: I thought he might get there first,
his regalia. His priest had shown the lay
of the land. But when the old bag heard the noise
I was making she reached out her hand. I hissed   840
and bit it like a sacred snake and she drew
her hand back right away and wrapped herself up
in her blankets. She kept still until, panicked,
she broke wind, sending up a stink like a skunk's.
I wolfed down a big chunk of stew and only stopped
when I was stuffed.

WIFE

Didn't the god come out to you?

CARIO

Not yet, but soon afterward when he was coming
our way I did something ridiculous: with a loud report
I let out a fart. My stomach had more than it could hold.   850

WIFE

No doubt he was quite disgusted by this transaction.

CARIO

He wasn't, but his daughters were, who escorted him.
Iaso blushed, and Panacea held her nose, averting
her head. Frankly she was incensed by my perfumed gloom.

WIFE

And the god?

CARIO

It was no problem for him.

WIFE

You mean, this god's kind of a yokel?

CARIO

No; he just likes the aroma of shit.

WIFE

You're some character!

CARIO

After this I was so scared I hid away while he   860
did his rounds and diagnosed each case
conscientiously. A slave put a stone mortar
and pestle at his side.

WIFE

> A stone mortar?

CARIO

> No, not the vessel, the thing it holds.

WIFE

> Look, you character, if you were under the covers
> how could you see?

CARIO

> Right through the holes in my cloak, they're cape-acious.
> First he concocted a plaster paste to stick it on
> for Neocleides: acid fig juice, squills (a bulbous plant   870
> of the genus Scilla, with narrow leaves and bell-shaped
> flowers) blended in; soaked well in Sphettian vinegar.
> The stuff prepared, he turned the eyelids back
> so it would smart even harder. The patient
> let out a yell and jumped up screaming, trying
> to get out of there. But the god just smiled
> and said "Sit down, and keep that plaster on.
> This will stop your faking an excuse to fail
> to show up at the Assembly session."

WIFE

> How very patriotic and wise this god is.   880

CARIO

> Next he went and sat down beside Wealth,
> holding Wealth's head in his hands. And then,
> taking a clean towel, he wiped the eyes all over
> carefully. The god's daughter, I can't remember
> whether it was Iaso . . . no, it was Panacea,
> covered his head and face with a purple cloth.
> The god hissed and two huge snakes came out
> from the temple in a rushing slide.

WIFE

    Holy smoke! Snakes!

CARIO

    They slipped noiselessly under the purple cloth   890
    and licked his eyes. At least, that's how it looked
    to me. And let me tell you, my lad, before you'd have time
    to drink ten cups of wine, Wealth stood right up:
    his sight was restored. I gave him a good round
    of applause and called the master; but instanter
    the god and both snakes had disappeared back inside
    the shrine. You can imagine the hearty reception
    Wealth received from those lying near him, and how
    they stayed up all the rest of the night until dawn.
    I was overflowing with praise for what the god had done   900
    to make Wealth able to see again so soon; plus, he made
    Neocleides even blinder than before.

WIFE

    Oh, Lord and masterpiece theater of the healing arts,
    Yours is the power! Now, where is Wealth?

CARIO

    On his way home. He's picked up an enormous crowd
    around him: all folks who've been perfectly honest
    in the past, but lacked the wherewithal, well they all
    greeted him and hailed him with high-five joy.
    Wealthy fat cats, the property owners who amassed
    their substance by dubious deals, had sullen looks and   910
    were surly and discountenanced.
    The poor, wearing wreaths, came on behind,
    laughing and shouting out victory songs;
    old men's rhythmic steps tapped out the beat.
    Soooo: all of you, come now, join up, and dance
    together: eight, skate, and celebrate. When
    you go home you won't be hearing the refrain
    "There's no more bread again!"

WIFE

    I'd like to wrap you up in a lot of loaves
    for bringing us such good news.   920

CARIO

    Don't hesitate. The crowd must be nearly at our gate.

WIFE

    All right. I'll go in and get a few handfuls
    of figs and nuts to bring down a shower
    of blessings on those newly discovered, recovered eyes.
(enters the house)

CARIO

    Yes, do.
(He goes out to meet the crowd at the gates. Music, and dance steps by
               the Chorus. The revelry stops as Wealth arrives.)

WEALTH

    To the Sun, first: Greetings and salutations!
    Then, to the somber soil of Athens, and the whole
    territory of Athens, which has welcomed me.
    I'm ashamed of my past doings, associated as I was
    with such men as I did, and avoiding familiarity   930
    with the deserving sort, out of sheer ignorance.
    Just think of it! Wrong in what I did as well
    as what I didn't do! But from now on this will all
    be reversed and I'll show everyone that it was
    against my own will to consort with bad characters.
(Chremylus enters, trying to get out of the clutches of the crowds who
            have heard that Wealth is coming to his house.)

CHREMYLUS

    Ugh! The hell with you! What a drag, these friends
    who suddenly show up when things are going well with you.
    They jab you, bruise your shins, each one of them
    intent on showing you how fond he is of you.

And who hasn't piped up? Is there a crowd of fogies   940
who haven't swarmed around me in the market square?
(Wife reenters from the house with the nuts and figs.)

WIFE

Ah, welcome, my darlings, both of you! This is
our old-fashioned way of showering you with greetings.

WEALTH

Well, don't. Since this is the very first house
I'm entering since getting back my sight
it's only right that I ought to bring something in
instead of taking it away.

WIFE

You won't accept our coming home presents?

WEALTH

Yes. But inside by the hearth. And that way
we can skip the spectacle. It's beneath the dignity   950
of the dramatist to scatter dried figs and sweetmeats
among the audience, for laughs.

WIFE

How right you are! Look at Dexinicus over there,
standing up to catch some figs.
(They go into the house. There is a musical interlude as the Chorus
resume their dance steps. After a while Cario comes
out of the house.)

CARIO

How sweet it is to prosper, my friends,
at no expense to oneself. A mountain of blessings
has been heaped up on this house—though we
haven't done any wrong. The meal chest is full

of white flour, our wine jars up to the brim
with dark, red wine, scented. Our large containers   960
are stuffed with silver and gold. Makes you wonder.
Our oil jars are full, our flasks with perfume.
The attic is crammed with figs. Every cruet for vinegar,
every pot, every dish has been transformed
to brass. Our rotten, crusty platters are now made of silver,
so you don't see the worn places; the lamp is ivory
all of a sudden. We don't wipe ourselves with stones, but
always have at hand some garlic stalks. And we underlings
play put and take with gold coins. At the moment,
our master is sacrificing a pig, a goat, and a ram   970
in the house, wearing a wreath on his head.
It's so holy smokey in there I had to come out. My eyes
were watering so badly I couldn't see anything.

(An honest man enters followed by a slave carrying a ragged cloak and a
pair of shoes.)

HONEST MAN

Come along, boy, so we can find the god.

CARIO

Ah, who's this coming now?

HONEST MAN

Someone who's seen hard times but is now well off.

CARIO

It would seem, then, that you're one of the better types.

HONEST MAN

Quite right.

CARIO

So what is it you're after now?

HONEST MAN
I've come to see the god. I have a lot   980
to thank him for. I had inherited a good piece
of property from my father and I used the income
from that to help my friends who were in need.
I thought of this as a useful means of spending
what I had.

CARIO
I'll wager your money disappeared fast enough.

HONEST MAN
Quite right.

CARIO
And then the hard times set in.

HONEST MAN
Quite right. I thought that if I were ever in need
of help I'd have good friends in those that I   990
had helped out when they needed it. But they
were no longer available: they turned away
and turned me away, and couldn't be seen anymore.

CARIO
Probably laughing at you?

HONEST MAN
Quite so. My safe deposit boxes, emptied out,
brought me to ruin.

CARIO
But you're not ruined now.

HONEST MAN
That's precisely why, and quite right too,
I've come here to extend my greetings and salutations
to the god responsible.   1000

CARIO

But what is that threadbare cloak your servant is carrying
for? What does it have to do with the god?

HONEST MAN

It's for a votive offering to him.

CARIO

Surely that's not the outfit you wore for your Bar Mitzvah?

HONEST MAN

No, it's what I've been shivering in for thirteen years.

CARIO

How about those shoes?

HONEST MAN

They've seen me through the cruel winters.

CARIO

So you've come to offer them too?

HONEST MAN

Indubitably.

CARIO

Pretty presents for the god! 1010
(A common informer enters, accompanied by his witness.)

INFORMER

What rotten luck! What wrack and wruin!
I'm three times, no, make that four, no, five,
no, twelve, no, ten thousand times unlucky. Heck!
I'm a wreck. My wine of good luck can be saturated
with water!

CARIO

    Apollo, and the other gods up there: what is
    the terrible evil this man has suffered?

INFORMER

    Yes, isn't it just, though! Everything gone
    out of my house. And it's this god to blame:
    if there's any justice he will be blind again.   1020

HONEST MAN

    I think I know now what's wrong. If someone
    around here has fallen on hard times, he has to be
    the worst sort of person.

CARIO

    Well then: thank *goodness* he's come to ruin.

INFORMER

    Where, where is he who promised he'd make us all
    rich men again as soon as he could see again?
    The fact is he's done his best to ruin some of us.

CARIO

    But who are all these people?

INFORMER

    Well, I'm one of them.

CARIO

    Renegades, house-breakers-into?   1030

INFORMER

    Zounds and Zeus! Your people don't have a scrap
    of good in you. It's you that must have my money.

CARIO

> By Demeter, this informer's got some crust!
> Look at the way he's swaggering in here.
> He's obviously dying for some food.

INFORMER

> You'd better race off to the agora.
> You're expected there to be turned and twisted
> on the wheel until you confess
> to all your misdoings.

CARIO

> Better look out for yourself.   1040

HONEST MAN

> O Zeus, our guardian: all the Greeks
> will owe you a great debt if this god
> of ours brings these lying informers
> to a bad end.

INFORMER

> Oh goodness migraine! So you're having a laugh
> at our expense? Or how did you happen to come by
> that cloak? The one I saw you in yesterday
> was plenty threadbare.

HONEST MAN

> Foo on you. And how do you like this ring?
> I bought it from Eudemus, one drach only.   1050
> It's a charm against snakebite.
> *(Cario takes a look at the ring.)*

CARIO

> I don't see any engraving "use against snakebite."

INFORMER
>This is really the outer limit. Here are you two,
>making fun of us but never saying what you're up to.
>Not saying what you're doing. You're up to no good.

CARIO
>Well, let's say we're not out to do you any good.
>I swear, I wish you'd both burst open, you
>and that witness with you, chock full of emptiness.

INFORMER *(sniffing)*
>You deny, you mutts, that inside there
>there's plenty of fish slices and roast meat?   1060
(keeps sniffing)
>Mmmm: that smells good.

CARIO *(to honest man)*
>Can you smell anything, old boy?

HONEST MAN
>The cold is the pits: his armpits, in that piece
>of tattered cloak he's wearing.

INFORMER
>Gods on high, how long must I let these foul
>insults rain down on me? I'm snowed.
>My head is bowed to realize how ill I fare,
>a fine, patriotic man like me.

CARIO
>Did you say fine, patriotic?

INFORMER
>If ever a man was.   1070

HONEST MAN
>Well, then: answer some of these questions.

INFORMER
> Questions?

HONEST MAN
> Are you an informer?

INFORMER
> You think I'd be such a fool?

HONEST MAN
> A business man?

INFORMER
> Yes: that is, I pretend to be one when it counts.

HONEST MAN
> What else? Oh, yes, have you learned any trade?

INFORMER
> Oh, spare me that.

HONEST MAN
> If you don't do anything, how do you live?

INFORMER
> I supervise everything, private and public.   1080

HONEST MAN
> And why?

INFORMER
> That's my profession: keep up with the news.

HONEST MAN
> What a house-breaker-into you are. How can you
> be an honest man when you're loathed for poking
> your nose into other people's business?

INFORMER
> Dumb bunny. Is it interfering when I'm only
> doing my best to help out the state?

HONEST MAN
> You have to cook up some plan, to "help out"?

INFORMER
> "Help" means support the laws on the books
> and not let them be broken.   1090

HONEST MAN
> Aren't the state-appointed judges supposed
> to do that?

INFORMER
> But who does the accusing?

HONEST MAN
> Those who are well informed.

INFORMER
> That's my identity: all state affairs
> revolve around me.

HONEST MAN
> Well, if that's the case, the leaders of the state
> are in a sorry state. Could you, wouldn't you,
> rather live a quiet life without having to work?

INFORMER
> You recommend an ovine existence, nothing to do   1100
> but bleat like a sheep, and sleep.

HONEST MAN
> And you wouldn't settle for that?

INFORMER
> Not even if you showered me with the rarest
> luxuries: the silphium of Battus, for example,
> plus Wealth himself.

CARIO
> Hurry up, now, take off your cloak.

HONEST MAN *(to informer)*
> He means you.

CARIO
> Then take off your shoes.

HONEST MAN
> Meaning you.

INFORMER
> One of you just try it, come on, if you're in shape!   1110

CARIO
> Shape's what I'm in.
> *(They grab the informer and strip off his cloak and shoes. The witness
> runs away.)*

INFORMER
> Hear ye, hear ye! They're stripping me, right out here
> in broad daylight!

CARIO
> You're not supposed to butt into everybody
> else's business.

INFORMER
> Hey, witness mine, can't you see what's going on?

CARIO

He's gone on, exported, that witness you imported.

INFORMER *(in a quavering voice)*

Gosh, here I am all alone and in
the process of being robbed.

CARIO

And that makes you whine?   1120

INFORMER

OH MY GAWD!

CARIO *(to honest man)*

Just give me your cloak to wrap
this slanderer in.

HONEST MAN

Nope, not this one. I dedicated it to Wealth,
some time ago.

CARIO

But what better place for it is there than
furled around the person of this sorry version
of a human being? Wealth we should rather gift wrap
in dignified togs.
(He takes the cloak from the honest man and drapes the informer in it.)

HONEST MAN

Now, what about the shoes?   1130

CARIO

I'll nail them up on his forehead, as if
he were a real wild olive tree.

INFORMER

I'm leaving. I'm weaker, you're stronger.
But if I meet up with some *well-informed*

companion I'll make sure that this mighty god
gets punished, today, because as only one person,
he's bent on undermining democracy, without
the citizens' support in the Council or the Assembly.
(He runs off.)

HONEST MAN

So . . . betake your self to the baths, arrayed
in my full set of armor, and stand there out in front.   1140
I used to man that station in days past.

CARIO

But he'll be grabbed by the bathman in the place
it hurts most, and be thrown out. The moment he sees
who it is, the bathman will recognize him for a
total good-for-nothing.
(There is an interlude of music and dance by the chorus. As it ends, an
old lady enters. She is dressed in a flowery garment
and acts like a lovesick girl. An attendant carries
sweetmeats and cakes on a tray.)

OLD LADY

Maybe these kind old gentlemen can tell me
if this house we've reached is in fact the one
where this new god lives, or whether we've missed
the place entirely.

CHORUS LEADER

No, Miss, you haven't missed it, and besides   1150
you're so young, and so cute.

OLD LADY

I'll just call somebody from the house.

CHREMYLUS *(entering)*

No need, I've just come out myself. So:
tell me why you've come along.

OLD LADY

My good friend, I've been under a terrible strain.
Ever since that god showed up he's made my life
simply unbearable.

CHREMYLUS

Why? Were you a vicious gossip among the women?

OLD LADY

Heavens, no!

CHREMYLUS

Have you been drinking in the law court, while waiting   1160
to be called?

OLD LADY

You're kidding, but my harsh pains are serious.

CHREMYLUS

Well, hurry now, tell me what these pains amount to.

OLD LADY

Lend an ear. There was this boy in love with me,
a happy, handsome, and honest chap, even though
he was poor. Anything I wanted he would do
for me, charmingly, gracefully. And I'd do
the same for him.

CHREMYLUS

These wants of his . . . what sort of wants?

OLD LADY

Very few. And he held me in great respect.   1170
He might ask me for twenty drachs—to buy
a cloak—or eight, for a pair of shoes,
some cotton tank tops for his sisters,

a chiffon mantle for his mother, or, for instance,
four bushels of wheat.

CHREMYLUS

That's not very demanding, I must say. He seems
to have held you in the greatest respect.

OLD LADY

What he used to say was that he made these requests
not out of greed but out of love. Putting on
my cloak reminded him of me.   1180

CHREMYLUS

A kind of reversible love he must have had.
He could turn it on and off.

OLD LADY

But now it's completely off. This good-for-nothing guy
has changed his mind. When I brought him this cake
on the tray, and the sweetmeats, and whispered
in his ear that I'd come in the early evening . . .

CHREMYLUS

What happened?

OLD LADY

He sent the stuff back, plus the condition that I
never come to him again, and this further message:
"The soldiers of Miletus were once very brave men.   1190
But that was long ago."

CHREMYLUS

I guess he's not such a low type. Now that he's rich
he's lost his taste for lentil soup. Earlier, though,
thanks to his poverty, he'd eat everything, with relish.

OLD LADY

> But formerly, I swear by the two goddesses,
> Demeter and Kore, he'd be at my door every day.

CHREMYLUS

> To see the body carried out?

OLD LADY

> Of course not. He just liked to hear my voice.

CHREMYLUS

> Or rather, to get something out of it.

OLD LADY

> And if he saw me in trouble he'd pet me   1200
> and call me duckie and dovey.

CHREMYLUS *(aside)*

> And get a kick out of asking for some shoes.

OLD LADY

> When I rode in my carriage to the Great Mysteries,
> if anyone dared look at me, I was battered and bruised
> all day long, he was so jealous.

CHREMYLUS *(aside)*

> Maybe he liked to eat his meals alone.

OLD LADY

> Another thing: he said my hands were nice and smooth.

CHREMYLUS *(aside)*

> Of course, when they held out twenty drachs.

OLD LADY

> And that my skin was sweet and fragrant.

CHREMYLUS *(aside)*
  Filled brimful with Thasian wine   1210
  of the best vintage.

OLD LADY
  And my glancing eyes: how soft they looked.

CHREMYLUS *(aside)*
  The man was no fool. He knew how to get at
  and use up the substance of a raunchy old woman.

OLD LADY
  So, my good man, the god has been quite unfair.
  He said he'd help all those who had been wronged.

CHREMYLUS
  What should he be doing? Speak up, and then
  it will be done.

OLD LADY
  Justice here means treating well the person
  who has treated you well. Or else, he gets   1220
  no benefits whatsoever.

CHREMYLUS
  Didn't he pay you back every night?

OLD LADY
  He said he'd never leave me all my life.

CHREMYLUS
  All right, he said that. But he considers you dead.

OLD LADY
  Oh, I languish with anguish!

CHREMYLUS *(aside)*
    No, it seems to me you've gone to pot.

OLD LADY
    So thin you could draw me through a ring easily.
(aside)
        Well, if the ring was like a barrel hoop.
        Here he comes now, the very fellow I've been
        giving evidence about. It looks like he's back   1230
        from some kind of a party.
*(Young man enters carrying a torch; a crown rests tilting across his
                forehead.)*

CHREMYLUS
    Apparently. Notice that torch, and the wreath.

YOUNG MAN
    Have a nice day, everybody.

OLD LADY
    How do you mean that "nice"?

YOUNG MAN
    Well, old dear, I see your hair's gone quite gray.

OLD LADY
    Thanks for the insult.

CHREMYLUS
    You haven't seen her for some time, I presume.

OLD LADY
    Some time, you dope? He was at my place yesterday.

CHREMYLUS
    He's like the rest of us, sees better when drunk.

OLD LADY
>   Oh no. His manners have always been bad.   1240

YOUNG MAN *(approaching the old lady and looking at her face with the help*
of his torch)
>   Poseidon! Presiding god of the sea!
>   Ye gods of old age! A mass of wrinkles on her face!

OLD LADY
>   Eeeeek! Not so close with that torch!

CHREMYLUS
>   She's on the beam. If a single spark touched her,
>   she'd blaze up like a withered olive wreath.

YOUNG MAN
>   Got time for a little game?

OLD LADY
>   Where, you whacko?

YOUNG MAN
>   Here. Just take these nuts.

OLD LADY
>   What kids' game is this?

YOUNG MAN
>   Guessing how many teeth you have.   1250

CHREMYLUS
>   Let me in on it. I guess three, make that four.

YOUNG MAN
>   Pay up. She's got one grinder. That's it.

OLD LADY

> Beast! You're off your rocker, turning me
> into a wash basin in front of all these men!
> You'd improve with a good scrubdown.

CHREMYLUS

> Ah, no: she's all dressed up to be put on sale.
> But scrape off that white-lead paint, and then
> she's one network of wrinkles, plain to see.

OLD LADY

> Not me, you miserable mutt.

CHREMYLUS

> You can't be in your right mind, old lady.   1260
> But I can't let this young man detest this young girl.

YOUNG MAN

> I'm so in love with her.

CHREMYLUS

> But she's bringing charges against you.

YOUNG MAN

> On what grounds?

CHREMYLUS

> On grounds of impudence. For saying "The soldiers of Miletus
> were once very brave, but that was long ago."

YOUNG MAN

> I don't intend to fight over her with you,
> because I respect your age. I wouldn't let another man
> get away with it, though. Just take the girl, now,
> and take off. Good luck!   1270

CHREMYLUS

Oh, I get it. You don't find it worthwhile to keep
company with her anymore.

OLD LADY

And that's going to be allowed?

YOUNG MAN

I'm not having anything to do with someone who
has been embraced these past thirteen thousand years.

CHREMYLUS

But you drank down the wine and found it fine;
might as well down the dregs.

YOUNG MAN

They're old and moldy, those dregs.

CHREMYLUS

You could remedy that with a strainer.

YOUNG MAN

I think we should go in. I want to dedicate   1280
this crown I'm wearing to the god.

OLD LADY

I have something to tell him, too.

YOUNG MAN

In that case I don't go in.

CHREMYLUS

Go ahead; she won't hurt you.

YOUNG MAN

Thanks for the accident assurance. But I've been
slapping tar on that old boat long enough.

OLD LADY
    You first; I'll follow you.

CHREMYLUS
    Good lord, she's got a grip on that guy!
    Hangs on him like a limpet.
*(They enter the house and the door is shut. After a brief interlude of
                music, Hermes enters, knocks at the door, and
                ducks back to hide.)*

CARIO *(opening the door)*
    Who's knocking? What's doing?   1290
    Nothing doing, I guess. The door will pay for this causeless
                creaking.
(He starts to close the door as Hermes calls out to him.)

HERMES
    Cario, stop it! Stop, Cario!

CARIO
    So it's you, is it? Were you the one banging
    on the door?

HERMES
    No. I meant to, but then you opened it. Race in
    and call your master out; then his wife, and his kids,
    and the servants, and then the dog, and then
    yourself, and then the sow.

CARIO
    For why? Tell me.

HERMES
    You rascal, Zeus plans to mix you all up in the   1300
    same bowl and throw you all together
    into the Barathrum.

CARIO
    What the heck is a Barathrum?

HERMES
>   A pit, you nit.

CARIO
>   For bad news like this the herald usually has his tongue
>   cut out.

HERMES
>   But you've committed the foulest of all felonies.
>   Ever since Wealth began seeing, no one has offered
>   a single thing to us gods: no frankincense,
>   no laurel, no barley cakes, no slaughtered beasts,   1310
>   *Nada!*

CARIO
>   And there'll be nothing coming your way. In time past,
>   after all, you did not look after us . . .

HERMES
>   I'm not so interested in the other gods;
>   as for me I'm completely ruined.

CARIO
>   Now you make sense . . .

HERMES
>   In former days, as dawn came up, the barmaids offered
>   all sorts of nice things to me: cake laced with wine,
>   honey, figs, and other things on the menu that Hermes
>   loves to eat. Nowadays I sit around with my feet up,   1320
>   doing nothing, famished.

CARIO
>   Reciprocal justice: you've had things from
>   others and then turned around and penalized them.

HERMES
>   Ah, woe is me! Woe is the cheesecake, fresca
>   ogni mercoledi!

CARIO

>And a tough dolce vita to you. No cakes *whatsoever*.

HERMES

>Gosh, I really used to like ham a lot.

CARIO

>Jump up and hang in the air by your own hams.

HERMES

>Oh woe, alas, I enjoyed those hot kidneys!

CARIO

>And now your kidneys are giving you trouble.   1330

HERMES

>Alas, oh woes! Half and half: half water, half wine!

CARIO

>Take a sip of this good open air, and you're off.

HERMES

>Could you do your fellow slave a favor?

CARIO

>Yes, if it's in my power to perform.

HERMES

>From the sacrificial feast you're preparing in the house,
>could you bring me some hot baked bread, or a slice
>of meat?

CARIO

>There's no take-out.

HERMES

>But I'm not called Hermes the Thief for nothing.
>Remember how, whenever you sneaked something   1340
>of your master's, you never got caught.

CARIO

> Yes, you sneak-thief, the deal being that if something
> tasty like a well-baked cake appeared you'd share
> in the proceeds.

HERMES

> Yes, and then you ate the whole thing yourself.

CARIO

> What you didn't share were the beatings I got
> when I was caught in the act.

HERMES

> Now you're triumphant, but don't take it out on me.
> Look on me as a shareholder, and take me in.

CARIO

> You'll leave the gods' realm and stay down here?   1350

HERMES

> Yes. Things are much better with you.

CARIO

> But that's AWOL, or even desertion.

HERMES

> Your native land is where you live well.

CARIO

> But then, what use would you be to us down here?

HERMES

> I'm the doorpost god. I could be the turnkey.

CARIO

> Posted at the door to turn the key? We don't need
> any turnkeys here.

HERMES

There's always the fact that I'm the god of business.

CARIO

The fact is: we've got our wealth. Why should we
shelter a fast-talking pitchman here?   1360

HERMES

I'm also the god of guile.

CARIO

Mmm, guile? That's not our style any more. We're honest.

HERMES

There's the fact that I'm the god who guides.

CARIO

We now have a god who sees. We don't need a god
who guides any longer.

HERMES

I'll settle for god of games. What do you say
to that? To fund competitions for athletic events
and endow the arts is surely an appropriate duty
for Wealth?

CARIO

It must feel good to attach one's name   1370
to such a long list of things. This person
has carved out a profession for himself. No wonder
our citizens busy themselves trying to get their name
on so many jury lists.

HERMES

Am I accepted then, in terms of these terms?

CARIO
   Yes, you're in. Now take these innards to the well
   and wash them well, so you can play your servant's role
   immediately.
(They enter the house. There is a brief musical interlude. A priest of
Zeus, a Salvation Army general, enters.)

PRIEST
   Can anyone tell me where Chremylus is?

CHREMYLUS *(coming out of the house)*
   Sir, General, sir, what is it?   1380

PRIEST
   Bad news. What else could it be? Ever since Wealth
   began to see, I've been dying of hunger. I'm the
   priest of Zeus, the one in charge of Salvation.
   But I don't have anything to eat.

CHREMYLUS
   What in heaven's name would be the cause of that?

PRIEST
   No one deigns to sacrifice any more.

CHREMYLUS
   Why is that?

PRIEST
   They're all rich. Previously, when they had nothing,
   a merchant, for instance, would make an offering
   for his safe return; or if a man was acquitted   1390
   in a court case, he would make a thanksgiving contribution;
   another might offer a sacrificial feast. As the priest
   for Salvation, I would be summoned. But now
   nobody . . . well, they don't just sacrifice nothing.
   No one comes around, except to use the rest rooms.

CHREMYLUS
Well, you get a fee for that, don't you?

PRIEST
What I think I should do is: resign from the service
to Zeus and put in for a job here.

CHREMYLUS
Don't worry about it. If God is willing, all will
be willing. After all, the God of General Salvation   1400
is right here on this spot. Here. He. You.

PRIEST
Tell me about it.

CHREMYLUS
We will now reestablish at once—but wait . . .
stay here—Wealth is where he was always stationed
before as the Treasury's eternal guardian,
in the Parthenon. So let's go! Bring out the torches!
(*The people from the house begin to assemble out front. Procession
assembles. One man brings torches.*)

CHREMYLUS (*to the priest*)
You take them. And head up the parade.

PRIEST
Yes, that's my profession.

CHREMYLUS
Someone go and tell Wealth to come along.
(*Music. As the procession forms, Wealth is escorted from the house. The
old lady comes bustling out.*)

OLD LADY
What am I supposed to do?   1410

CHREMYLUS
> Take these pots of lentil soup we're bringing
> to the re-installation, and carry them on your head
> in solemn dignity. It's lucky you're wearing that
> dress with the spots on it.

OLD LADY
> But what about the reason I came here?

CHREMYLUS
> All in order. The chap will visit you tonight.

OLD LADY
> All right. If you promise he'll come to me,
> I'll carry these pots.

CHREMYLUS
> Wow, these pots are not like your usual pots,
> scummy on the bottom. These have the scum on the top.   1420
> *(Music. The actors march in triumph toward the Acropolis, where they*
> *will install Wealth in the Treasury of Athens again.*
> *The chorus follows, singing.)*

CHORUS
> WE WON'T STAND HERE ON THE STAGE ANY LONGER
> BUT FLY IN THEIR WAKE, LIKE SONGBIRDS.

About the Translators

FRED BEAKE was born in Cheshire in 1948, grew up in the rural West Riding, and has lived in Bath since 1972. He is the author of several books of original poetry and translations, including *The Whiteness of Her Becoming, The Fisher Queen,* and *Places and Elegies.* In addition to his work as a poet, he has written critical works on Shelley and H.D. and has published numerous articles and reviews in *Acumen,* the *Green Book,* and the *New Statesman.* His translations include works by Horace, Catullus, and Alcuin. Since 1990 he has served as the main poetry reviewer for *Stand* and is currently coeditor of the magazine *Poet's Voice.*

PALMER BOVIE, Professor Emeritus of Classics, Rutgers University, has published many translations of the classics, including works of Virgil, Horace, Cicero, Martial, Plautus, and Lucretius. Educated at Lawrenceville School and Princeton University, he received his Ph.D. from Columbia University and has taught at Columbia, Princeton, Indiana University, and the American Academy in Rome. With David R. Slavitt, he served as coeditor of the Complete Roman Drama in Translation Series, in which several of his own translations appeared.

JACK FLAVIN writes and translates poetry for numerous academic journals, including *Classical Outlook, Modern Age, Cimmaron Review,* and *Appalachia Quarterly.* He has coedited *Poulty: A Magazine of Voice,* serving as principal editor for eleven years. A veteran of World War II, he went on to graduate from the University of Maryland, and later received his Master of Foreign Studies from the University of Zurich and his M.S. in Library Science from Drexel Tech.

DAVID R. SLAVITT, poet, novelist, critic, and journalist, has published sixty books. His translations include works of Virgil, Ovid,

Seneca, Avianus, Prudentius, Statius, Claudian, Bacchylides, and Ausonius. His fifteenth volume of original poetry, *PS3569.L3*, appears in 1998. He served as coeditor with Palmer Bovie of the Complete Roman Drama in Translation series.